Donnie Maib is a leader of leaders. I've known him since I was 18 years old, but it was what happened after I met him that changed everything. Donnie Maib pushed me past what I thought was possible and helped me to understand what it takes to be an exceptional leader. His selflessness, fearlessness and servants' heart will help transform you and your team. Whether it was national championships or bustling professional careers, Donnie Maib was the brain behind it all. I can't wait for you to check this book out and learn what I learned. The leadership isn't always easy, but it's always worth it.

—SAM ACHO
Author, Motivational Speaker, ESPN Analyst

Coach Maib combines tested leadership methods with strategies gleaned from his unique experience at the highest echelon of sports. *The Secret Sauce of Leadership* is required reading for anyone who is committed to elevating their capacity to lead others.

—DARON K. ROBERTS
Coach, Author, and Speaker

As a two-time National Championship coach, understanding and implementing leadership strategies are key components to developing individual and team success. Donnie is a master leadership coach, who I lean on daily, to help me, my captains and team grow. As a coach, I must know the way so I can develop and show my athletes the way these "secret sauce" principles are staples to our championship program.

—JERRITT ELLIOTT
Volleyball Head Coach, University of Texas

Donnie is an incredible coach, motivator, and leader! He has made a huge impact on our leadership program we developed in our company and his message translates from the court to the board room, to the family dinner table! Not only that, but he's an incredible guy with a passion to help others succeed. His down to earth, fun, and relatable style makes his leadership's principles truly enjoyable to learn. Thank you, Donnie, for all that you have taught myself and our team!

—ALLY DAVIDSON
Founder & CEO of Camp Gladiator

In all my life no one has had as profound an impact on my life as a Coach, husband, father, and man than Donnie Maib!! I shared an office with Donnie for many years and it was truly a blessing. The lessons learned from him not only in countless conversations but also by his living out his leadership lessons daily. Donnie is a servant leader with a warrior's heart! A compassionate soul whose spirit blazes with passion!! Truly a man for all seasons whose leadership style is one that is relational, genuine and can reach anyone anywhere right where they are!! This book is a must have for coaches, business owners, parents, anyone who has people that look to them for leadership and guidance this is the one. I know 1st hand the impact that Donnie had and has on me and my family. Truly a blessing to all he touches. I'm proud of the work he has put into this book. You will be moved. I'm also honored to call him a friend and a brother.

—COACH TIM CROSS
University of North Carolina

I've known Donnie Maib for years and everyone that has been around him as an athlete-coach and coworker says the same thing, he's an even better person and in this book, you'll see why he is so beloved and respected by so many across a vast landscape. Coach Maib lays out how to lead and elevate others around you, how to be the defining force in someone's life and to help them become the best version of themselves.

—MATT DURANT
Head Strength & Conditioning Coach, University of La Verne

I have worked with Donnie for over seventeen years with champion athletes at Texas, so I have seen firsthand his exemplary work as a high-performance coach and leadership mentor. Fortunately, he has included these best practices in *The Secret Sauce of Leadership*. Now, you can learn what the Longhorns do about transformative leadership principles and practices, from Coach D himself.

—DR. MIKE VOIGHT
Author, Leadership Consultant, Professor Physical Education and Human Performance Central Connecticut State University

Donnie Maib is no stranger to the subject of leadership. As a Director of Olympic Sports Athletic Performance, he has taken his teams to great heights competitively as well as teaching young leaders how to win, lose, and lead others. He not only molded leaders, but he is also a terrific teacher on leadership. Most of all he is a stellar model of what a great leader looks and acts like. If you are needing a refresher on leadership, this is a book you need to read, as does your team. It is practical and provides depth and what it means to lead from the heart and with strength of character.

—DEBORAH LEVERETT
Enterra-Partners President

Donnie Maib has channeled more than three decades of experience to write a timely and relevant book that every current and emerging leader should read. Powerful and practical, Donnie shares insight on his journey to success and provides his keys to becoming an extraordinary leader. Everyone's recipe for success should include his "Secret Sauce!"

—ALLEN HARDIN
Chief Medical Officer, The University of Texas

One of my favorite people and an elite leader, Donnie Maib delivers with his new book *The Secret Sauce of Leadership.* Donnie has the unique ability to take high level leadership principles and make them stick with his down to earth humility and humor. Do yourself, your family, and your organization a favor and grab this resource as fast as you can.

—RON MCKEEFERY, MA, MSCC, RSCC*E
Head Strength and Conditioning Coach University of Washington
Collegiate Strength and Conditioning Coach of the Year (2008) (2016)
International Coach of the Year (2020)

THE SECRET
SAUCE
OF LEADERSHIP

DONNIE MAIB

Cover & interior design by Typewriter Creative Co.
Graphics by Vectonauta via Freepik

Scriptures taken from the Holy Bible, New International Version®, NIV®. Copyright © 1973, 1978, 1984, 2011 by Biblica, Inc.™ Used by permission of Zondervan. All rights reserved worldwide. www.zondervan.com The "NIV" and "New International Version" are trademarks registered in the United States Patent and Trademark Office by Biblica, Inc.™

ISBN 979-8-9890672-1-3 (Paperback)
ISBN 979-8-9890672-5-1 (Hardcover)
ISBN 979-8-9890672-0-6 (eBook)

DEDICATION

In loving memory of my sister
Kimberly Lane Maib (6/27/65 – 3/15/23).
*I miss you very much and will cherish all the
memories of you. Thank you for teaching me that
true unconditional love is sincerely loving people
no matter what the circumstance is.*

CONTENTS

Introduction... 11

1 | Attitude 15

2 | Mentality.. 25

3 | Professionalism 39

4 | Authenticity 57

5 | Competence 61

6 | Career Stallers and Stoppers 79

7 | Personal Development 95

8 | Mistakes and Mess Ups 111

Conclusion: Leadership Navigation 129

Endnotes 135

Acknowledgments................................... 139

About the Author 143

INTRODUCTION

The alarm sounded at 4:30 a.m. My dream morphed into a nightmare. I sat up on the edge of the bed in my boss' guest room, staring at the floor while I contemplated my escape. If I got up a little earlier and headed back to Tennessee, no one would ever notice. I could steal away in the middle of the night. My car was still packed and, by this time tomorrow, I could be home. I had accepted my first paid internship as a strength coach at the University of Colorado at Boulder under the direction and guidance of E. J. "Doc" Kreis, and reality was hitting me hard. I was in my second week of work, rising before dawn and coming home well after dinner, this would-be dream job had lost its appeal quickly.

Doc was an early riser and to this day I don't know if he ever slept. He was always full of energy, and I swore he took naps with one eye open. I was a recent University of Georgia graduate, having spent several seasons playing college football. While having people wait on me hand and foot as a football player was fun, I was not prepared for the role of an intern. The roles were flipped. I was no longer the one being served, I was serving others. It was no longer about me. Going from the pinnacle of college sports with its adulation and praise, to sitting exhausted in your boss' guest room, makes you think some crazy thoughts.

This wasn't what I signed up for. The opportunity sounded much more glamorous when I first started telling others about it. Launching a coaching career at the University of Colorado was an opportunity you didn't pass up. I struggled for years in college trying to figure my career path. Like most athletes, I had dreams of playing professionally, and so I refused to consider a career outside of sports.

A tragic injury in my senior year changed the trajectory of my life. I tore my ACL in preseason, and in those days, a torn ACL was pretty much the kiss of death to an athletic career. The technology and resources to get you back to top shape didn't exist then. I spent hours upon hours rehabbing my injured knee, but it was never quite the same. I ended up not being able to play until the last three games. That entire year was one of the darkest, most challenging times of my life. My dream of playing in the NFL was shattered. My identity was lost and my future seemed bleak. I still remember sitting in the locker room all alone after we beat Ohio State in the Citrus Bowl, not wanting to take off my uniform, knowing it would be the last time I would suit up. With no direction in my life after football, the next months ahead seemed hopeless. I was depressed, lost and confused, with no idea of what to do next. It was during that season that I remembered a conversation with a mentor about getting into coaching. It sparked some much needed hope. Coaching seemed like the next best step for me to take. I took the opportunity thinking it would be an easy transition. Man, I was wrong.

I will never forget sitting on the edge of the bed that day. It was a defining moment, forcing me to stare reality in the face and not back down. Early morning workouts, long hours, little to no appreciation, and extremely low pay was my new lot in life. That morning, staring at the red glow of the digital clock, I had to make a decision. Will I commit? Can I continue? Do I have what it takes to be a college strength coach? Is this something I want to do my whole life? Where will this even take me? I was filled with doubt and dread. After reflection and deep thought, I came to my senses. There was no way I could quit; no way I could turn back. I had to go on. In that moment, I decided to not disappoint my friends, family, and mainly, myself. I put one foot on the floor and then the other. I got dressed, grabbed the keys to my 1988 Bronco II, and headed into work. Looking back now, I appreciate those days. They were hard, but they were good for me. Struggle isn't bad. Struggle is often not only good, but needed for growth. For the next two years, I endured many hard times while interning. No money, no life, difficulties with staff and athletes, and a multitude of personal problems I had to work through as I limped my way into my calling as a strength coach.

Looking back, I can see clearly now what I could not see then. The internship made me stronger, helping me mature as a young leader. I gained perspective on life I could not have acquired any other way. My character was forged and my values were fleshed out in those early years of coaching.

Nothing worth having comes easy. Though technology is getting exponentially faster and life is picking up speed, you cannot take shortcuts in your character and career. Slow and solid, fast and fragile is a mantra I espouse. Starting out in your career is not usually glamorous and exciting. It may not be what you expected or start the way you thought it should have, but you will get to a place where you enjoy what you do. That's what this book is about: the nuances and intricacies of leadership. Taking the lessons you learn as you work through struggles and successes, and applying them uniquely to your situation. That will be your secret sauce. Your path will be different than everyone else and that is ok. In my wildest dreams I would never have thought that morning, sitting on the edge of my boss' bed, that I would be the person I am today. Being a leader was nowhere in my mind. The crazy thing I know now as I look back, is that the seeds of leadership were there the whole time, I just couldn't see them. It's easy to see the position you want, but it is very difficult to fathom the problems and processes you will have to go through to be prepared for it. We overestimate the glamor of the position we seek to attain and we underestimate the value of the process that will get us there. This book will look into all the different facets and aspects you will encounter and go through on your leadership journey.

CHAPTER 1

ATTITUDE

"Attitude determines the altitude of life."

—

EDWIN LOUIS COLE

The Best Followers Make the Best Leaders

Growing up, I loved playing the game *Simon Says*. The pure simplicity of the game is part of what makes it fun. One person is designated as the leader who starts the game by saying "Simon Says" followed by an action. For example, "Simon says, touch your nose." All others playing the game are followers, doing exactly what the leader says. To win the game, you must be the last person standing who did exactly what the leader, Simon, said to do. If you don't do what Simon says, you are out. You must focus intently on what the leader is saying, and if the leader doesn't use the words "Simon Says" before the command, you don't do it. It's that simple. The objective, and fun, of the game is to catch everyone doing something Simon didn't tell them to do. It takes great focus and listening skills to excel at the game. The best follower of the group wins the game. You would think as kids growing up playing *Simon Says* we would carry it over into our adult lives and careers but we don't. When it comes to our jobs, people don't always like doing what they are told. In the real world, Simon is your boss or supervisor and it isn't a game. If you mess up, it's not funny and you may not get another shot to play again.

I started consuming leadership books as a young coach. I wanted to be in charge. I wanted to be seen and viewed as a leader. I wanted the title, power, and pull. The more I studied leadership, the more I noticed something: if you want to be the best leader you can be, you need to be a great follower first. I'm not talking about being a 'yes' man or woman, but someone who understands effectively how authority and organizations work.

You don't arrive at a place of leadership overnight. You begin in lower positions where you have got to be really good at doing what you have been asked to do. In my early coaching years, there were times I didn't like getting told what to do, and even more times where I didn't do what was asked. I would wait until the last minute, or I would let someone else pick up the slack for me. The more I studied leadership, the more I understood being a great leader is all about getting things done promptly, and with excellence. As you become a person who can follow a good leader, you begin to build credibility and trust with others as a person who gets things done. Simply put, your influence will grow. John C. Maxwell defines leadership as influence, nothing more and nothing less.[1] As you follow others well, over time you earn the right to lead others because you have proven you are trustworthy. If you want to be a great leader, I encourage you to consider these principles of being a good follower.

1. **The Little Things** – attention to detail helps you stand out. Many people today do not do their jobs with excellence. If your boss or

supervisor asks you to do something, don't just complete the task, but do it well. If you are creating a report, double and triple check your work. If you are running an errand, be on time and get it done efficiently. If you are helping or serving someone for your boss, go the extra mile to do what you have been asked. It sends a message to the person you are helping that they are important, and word of your performance will eventually get back to your boss.

2. **Follow Through** – when asked to do something, finish the task. If necessary, create a system to ensure tasks get done. You not only lose credibility with your boss, but you also create the impression you cannot be counted on if you never follow through. Treat small and big assignments the same: get it done. Period.

3. **Study People** – great followers learn to study their supervisors. How do they like things done? How do they communicate? What lowers their stress and gives them confidence? What words do they use to influence and motivate others? When you learn how others think and behave, you can stay one step ahead and move quickly. Being a keen observer will greatly benefit your leadership.

4. **Sense of Urgency** – great leaders move fast. They are people of action and accomplishment. Matching your leader's sense of urgency makes you a good follower. One word of caution: don't get too far ahead of your boss. If you haven't built trust or established consistent communication, it can come back to bite you. Staying in step with your leader will be key to your success.

5. **Be a Lifter Not a Leaner** – there are two types of people: lifters and leaners. When a lifter comes into your team or organization, the boss and others can feel it right away. These are people who make everyone's job easier by picking up slack and carrying weight. You may not always realize it, but the load has gotten lighter. A leaner,

on the other hand, makes the work more difficult. When they do not do their job well, it impacts those around them. They need constant reminders or their work must be reassigned to others to get it done. As a good follower, you become a lifter and make other people's jobs easier.

If you intend to be the best leader you can be, you must take following others seriously especially early on. Understanding the many facets of leadership will aid you in the years to come. Over and over again, I have witnessed leaders who only give orders and refuse to take instruction. I caution against this behavior as it typically results in being a career staller or stopper. Inevitably, these type leaders run into someone with more power and influence who resists their leadership and refuses to work with them. Learning to follow first keeps you humble. Humility will be a guard against derailing your career. Address this early on and learn it well. Learning to follow may appear a weakness at first, but in the end you will know it for the strength it is.

Green and Growing or Ripe and Rotten

My parents got divorced when I was very young. Because they shared custody of me, I would alternate weekends staying at their homes. One weekend at my dad's, the next at my mom's. At my mom's house, there was a designated wall where she tracked my growth. I would stand with my back to the wall and she would place a small mark on the wall at the top of my head. When she first started tracking my growth, my visits took on a whole new meaning. I couldn't wait to see how much I had grown since my last visit. My excitement was dulled after I realized I wasn't growing at all, or at least that's what it felt like. To my surprise, when I remembered to check my growth after a longer span of time, the mark was a little higher than the last measurement. I didn't feel like I was changing at all, but when I saw the marks climbing the wall it made me feel alive because I knew I was growing and getting bigger. More than anything, I wanted to grow big and tall like my dad. He was 6'5" and weighed over 300 lbs. I was a little pipsqueak and any sign of growth got me excited.

Growth and improvement in our roles makes a significant difference as leaders. In nature, things that are growing and healthy are green, vibrant, and lush. Things that are dying wilt, brown, and rot. Dead things decay and deteriorate over time but living organisms expand, change in shape and size, and grow. I love the quote by Ray Kroc, the founder of McDonald's Corporation. "When you're green you're growing. When you're ripe you rot."[2] You are either getting better or getting worse. There is no in between. It is essential for you to adopt habits of continuous improvement if you want to lead one day. In today's leadership economy, those who consistently and strategically work to improve themselves have an edge over others. The job market is oversaturated with individuals who are qualified to fill a limited number of positions and it falls to you to make sure you are prepared once the right opportunity comes your way.

Growth is not always comfortable. During growth spurts, I would experience pain in my joints and body. These are commonly referred to as "growing pains," and the principle also applies to our careers. Career growth will not always be enjoyable, easy or evident. In his book, Leadership Pain, Sam Chand suggests that if we as leaders cannot handle the pain and problems we experience at one level, we will not advance to the next. He states, "You'll grow only to the threshold of your pain."[3] If you cannot handle the pain you are facing at your current level, you will not be ready for the next level. It will be harder.

There will also be times when growth is not evident until further down the road. It is during these times you need encouragement from others to persevere and not give up. The most difficult times we face in our leadership journey is having no proof or evidence of improvement. When growth is small and incremental, we can experience profound discouragement. When I would check my height on my mom's growth chart and not see the mark move, I was discouraged. Though I was not getting taller, internally I was growing and didn't realize it.

Trees have three primary ways in which they grow: upward and outward with more branches, downward with deeper roots, and inwardly with increasing sap. During the spring and summer, growth is quite visible in the new leaves and bigger branches. During the fall and winter, a tree sheds its leaves and looks like it's dying. It is during the silent season the tree's sap is increasing internally so it will be able to nourish the new growth coming soon. Two of the three ways a tree grows are not visible to the naked eye. Growth is occurring, but you don't see it happening. It's the same for our careers. There will be seasons when your growth is visible enough to notice and celebrate it. There will be winter seasons in your life where growth will be more internal and not as recognized. Perhaps your current job is more obscure than you'd prefer; no one sees the work you're doing, you don't get any recognition, but it matters how you do the work. Perhaps you are facing relational pressure or are constantly scrutinized by an oppressive supervisor or colleague, how you respond in these hard situations will determine how much you grow.

Another example of uncomfortable growth is staying in difficult situations. We can often build our perspective around the negative aspects, considering it "too hard". Often, only hindsight will help us realize how good a challenging season was for us. Some of the most challenging and difficult seasons and situations I endured provided me with the biggest growth and maturity opportunities. I wouldn't trade them for anything now. Going through them wasn't fun, but if I had run from the challenges, I wouldn't have been ready to take on bigger roles and responsibilities. Let's take a look at five ways to help you to continue to grow, get better, and improve as a leader.

1. Have Multiple Mentors for Different Areas of Your Life – the greatest artists in history didn't have online learning and videos. They learned and mastered their craft by learning from the masters. They learned by doing. Day in and day out they would apprentice themselves to their craft. Through time and practice, their skills would improve. The Master/Apprentice model was the primary way they developed a trade.

While it looks different today, the principle stands. If you want to ensure growth, look for multiple mentors for different aspects of your life. These could be financial, relational, fashion, career, parenting, leadership, or spiritual. Some considerations when seeking a mentor:

- Are they someone you want to emulate?
- Is any area of their life questionable or lacking integrity? If so, you may want to reconsider.

Pay attention to little things when selecting a mentor. Mentoring is not just about learning a skill from someone, you will also pick up on their habits and lifestyle to some degree too. Additionally, not all mentors are selected with intention. Meaning, there will be times you are placed in close proximity with someone who organically becomes your mentor. It wasn't planned or thought out, it happened because you were in the right place at the right time. Be alert for these types of situations because it may only last for a short season.

2. **Develop a Personal Growth Plan** – some growth in our lives will happen automatically, like growing taller, but most growth takes effort and purpose. Curate a list of your interests and gifts and make a strategic plan to develop those areas. What books, courses, podcasts, or experts can you glean from to support your improvement? Pick one or two subjects you want to do a deep dive on and study them. You would be surprised how fast you can learn when you focus on one subject for an extended period of time. As you come up with

your personal growth plan, make note of gaps you need to work on. Brainstorm how you will increase your knowledge and skills in that area.

3. **Bloom Where You Are Planted** – growth is a choice. You may be limited in your job, location, work space, resources, and time but you will have to choose to grow before it will happen. Anyone can come up with excuses and look for reasons why their growth isn't occurring, but if you really want to improve, bloom where you are planted. Find a way to improve yourself. Don't find time, make time. Your mentality and mindset can imprison you or empower you. You decide. I have seen some of the most beautiful flowers grow in the most difficult places.

4. **Embrace Difficult Seasons of Your Life** – I loved it when it would rain in the country growing up. Dark clouds warned of lightning, thunder, and high winds. Rain would pour down sideways. It would be scary at times with all the turbulence outside. Once the storm passed, there was such peace and calm. The air was cool and smelled so fresh. Sometimes a rainbow would appear and everything seemed alright. The anxiety over the storm gave way to peace. It's the same with difficult seasons in our lives. Going through hard times and challenging situations is stressful, dramatic, and unsettling but just like the storm, this too shall pass. When you are in the midst of a difficult season personally or professionally, weather the storm. Embrace it. Use adversity to strengthen your character, clarify your purpose, and raise your level of commitment. We need to be like the Hereford cattle.[4] Hereford cattle are known for how they face storms in the open prairie; while most cattle turn their backs to the freezing cold storms and are driven back into the fence lines where they eventually get trapped, pile up and die, Hereford cattle are known for standing shoulder to shoulder and walking into

the icy storm blast head on. By using this approach, Hereford cattle are most always found alive. In a season of difficulty, face the storm head on. Don't run from it or get driven back. Stand your ground.

5. **Use Every Disappointment as a Reappointment** – disappointments can knock you to your knees. Perhaps you didn't get the job, you made a huge mistake, or someone let you down. Moments like these test you. How you respond in these types of scenarios and situations will define you as a leader. If you cannot rise from small disappointments how will you handle something bigger? How we do anything is how we do everything. Our attitudes, habits, and actions shape how we think and view life. Often our struggle helps us grow the most. Disappointment can increase our motivation, dedication, and perseverance. The younger we are in our careers, the most painful growth we will encounter is maturity. Maturation is challenging because it takes time. Maturity doesn't always come with age; it begins with acceptance of responsibility. An indicator of maturity is viewing difficult situations as growth opportunities.

CHAPTER 2

MENTALITY

*"If you change the way you look at things,
the things you look at change."*

—

WAYNE DYER

Position Versus. Disposition

I hated one-on-one drills in football. Being matched with a teammate in practice while the coaches and other players circled around to see who could push the other around the most would win. Time after time, I was beaten or locked in a stalemate. One day, my coach looked at me and said, "Low man wins."

"Huh? Is that a riddle, coach?"

"No, son, low man wins! The lowest point of contact has the advantage."

The next time I went against a teammate, this was my sole objective. Sure enough, I bent my elbows and knees to get under my opponent when we collided. Success at last! Learning how to not get run over like a freight train was key to my future as a football player. It worked even better when I was outmatched against someone much larger. While I didn't win every time my success rate improved significantly.

The "position versus disposition" principle works similarly to the "low man wins" principle in football. Leadership is not about the title or responsibilities you hold, but about how you view your mindset, value, and vision towards the title and responsibilities. Another way I like to say it is "winning starts on the inside." If you view or see your position as small or insignificant, your impact will directly correlate to your mindset. If you see yourself as small, you will be small. If you view your position as vital and important, it can become that over time.

One of my good friends, Robert Dos Remedios, says, "Make your bigtime job the one you currently have!" Leaders always looking for the "bigtime" job never seem to find it. They see their current role as nothing more than a small stepping stone to a better future. Look, I get it... there are positions and organizations that lack resources, money, and staff, but that doesn't mean you use those as an excuse to do a mediocre job. Making your current job the one you are hoping for is a demonstration of disposition. Merriam-Webster defines *disposition* as your "prevailing tendency, mood, or inclination."[5] In other words, how you think, feel, and act towards your job sets the tone for your performance and results.

How is your mood at your current job? What are your tendencies? Are you lethargic, bored, and dreading work? That is your current disposition. You might be saying, "But Donnie, I don't have any support, my boss is horrible, my coworkers don't like me, and I have not gotten a raise in years!" I hear you, I do. I am not asking about them. I am asking about you. Even as leaders, we have only so much control over how others will act or what the administration will decide. We do have control over our disposition: our attitude, effort, and passion. If you need a visual for small things having a great impact, imagine a mosquito in a sleeping bag! In twenty-nine years of coaching, I have seen interns and entry-level positions who get paid next to nothing have more impact than some full time staff members. The interns had greater rapport with the athletes, got things done more quickly, studied more, and had more energy and excitement at work. They were a joy to work with. I have also seen experienced leaders who had greater levels of influence and respect compared to those in positions of pay higher than their own, all because they found ways to make an impact, evolve, stay relevant and adapt with current trends. They didn't fade out or become outdated. They maintained a good disposition throughout their career. How you view yourself and your role will impact your level of influence as well as your results.

Mason was an intern who emulated this principle. He interviewed for a voluntary position we had open, and while I don't recall our entire conversation, I remember walking away from the interview thinking, "I like this guy. He has a 'can do' spirit about him. I want to give him a shot." Mason was married with a couple of kids at the time, and got up at 4:00 am to drive to Austin from Killeen every morning, a 45 minute drive each way. He worked 12 hour days with no pay, while his wife carried the financial load for the family. I never saw Mason with a bad attitude or feeling sorry for himself during his internship. He had an amazing disposition. Over time he became someone who was very trustworthy and dependable for us. He got stuff done and the athletes loved him too, and so eventually he earned part time pay. His role expanded and his influence increased, which led him to obtaining a full-time position. Today he is a sought-after consultant and mentor for younger coaches. His disposition was the difference. Over time if you are able to maintain the right disposition, the sky will be the limit for you.

Let's consider five viewpoints you will need in regards to your disposition to help you succeed.

1. **How Bad Do You Want It** – the leaders who really want to lead will find a way. These leaders are persistent and prevailing in the face of adversity. I find there are more young leaders looking for big positions and unwilling to start small. When first starting out and learning to lead, oftentimes your first job will not be the one you wanted. It won't be perfect or convenient and you may not even enjoy it, but one of the greatest tests of leadership is doing things you may not want to do in order to make progress. In my industry, I have witnessed far too many coaches turn down opportunities to work because it wasn't in a city or with a team they liked. Early on in your career, always take opportunity over pay. Opportunities come in all shapes, sizes and colors. What you may snub your nose at might just be the opportunity you need to put you on a successful career path. Don't pass up an opportunity that seems too small. If you really want it bad enough it will show. When you first start out, the sacrifices will be big. You will not get paid much if at all. You will get a lot of tasks that seem menial or small. The hours you work will seem endless as well with very little reward. That's ok to start small but don't think small. Think big and you will not stay there as you progress.

2. **No Task Is Too Small** – are you above doing seemingly small, petty tasks? If so, you will struggle. I remember years ago we had an intern who got offended because we asked them to fold towels. They considered themselves above the task. They came to coach, not fold towels, and they didn't last long. Even today as I have moved up, any task or job I hand out I ask myself, 'Will I help with this task'? Any

assignment I delegate or hand out, I have first and foremost got to be willing to roll up my sleeves and get dirty too. If not, I am not modeling servant leadership. The tallest leaders must stoop to the lowest of jobs. They bend down and help others. Having a disposition of 'no task is too small for me' keeps you humble but it also keeps you connected and sets a great example for others to follow.

3. **No Problem Is Too Big** – problem solvers get promoted. Period. The person who comes up with solutions but also gets in the game and helps become part of the solution will always have a job. This is the big difference between whiners and winners. Whiners complain about all the challenges and problems, and they love to point out what's wrong and what's not working. They see limitless impossibilities. They are hopeless, despondent, and draining. Whiners are defeated by problems and challenges. There is no way to succeed now. "The ship will fail before it sails," whiners say. On the other hand, winners are energized by challenges and problems, and solution oriented. Their mantra is "The battle is won before the battle is begun". They will find a way to win. If you want to grow as a leader and move up over time, look at your disposition. Are you a whiner or winner?

4. **I Can Work With Anyone** – flexibility and adaptability are requirements for the future job market. Times are changing quickly and you must be flexible in who you work with and how you work with them. One of my favorite quotes is by Robert Ludium: "Blessed are the flexible, for they shall not be bent out of shape."[6] If you want to lead one day you must be flexible in your approach with people, especially demanding people. The more diverse group of people you work with, you more than likely interact with different viewpoints

and opinions of how things should be done. Don't get too caught up in how things should be done. "My way or the highway" will not get you very far. Imagine your mind like a parachute: if it's not open, it will not work. Be open minded to working with people who have different ideas than yours. Working with demanding and difficult people requires you to give a lot at first. Do it their way, see their views, and learn their style. As you give consistently, they will buy into you as a person and eventually you will earn their respect and they will start to want to know your thoughts and opinions. Being stubborn, close minded, and inflexible is not a beneficial disposition or attitude.

5. **My Role Is Bigger Than My Job Description** – I attended a Walt Disney World training program years ago and one of the key differences in how Walt Disney treats their employees is wrapped up in the job titles. All job titles are referred to as "characters". In other words, they are not just janitors, cooks, or cleaners. At any point, if any employee sees a patron, parent, or child needing help they are to stop what they are doing and attend to that person or family. They are "characters" in a bigger story in the park. Their role is bigger than their job description. I love that! What about you? How can your role serve and help those not in your department? Find creative ways to help others when you can. Get involved in marketing, ticketing, or human resources. Go above and beyond to get connected to the community around you. What gifts or talents do you have that can help someone near you? A little help goes a long way with others. Small keys open big doors.

Over the years I have had the pleasure and privilege of hiring staff for various types of roles and departments. I have seen incredibly competent employees come in and flounder. I have seen mediocre applicants come in and flourish. If I could summarize disposition in one sentence, it would be this: "Hire for attitude, train for skill". I would rather hire someone with a great attitude who lacks skill than bring in someone who is highly skilled with a bad attitude. It just doesn't work. Though it may take some time to get them up to speed, it will be much better in the long run. There will be fewer problems, higher morale, and more momentum built working with someone who has a great attitude and just needs some good mentoring. As the saying my coach told me years ago on the football field still holds true today in our jobs: "Low man wins!". Your disposition is more important than your position.

Leave a Big Hole

The largest sinkhole in the United States is located near Calera, Alabama. The Alabama Geological Survey estimates the hole at 300 feet wide, 325 feet long and 120 feet deep. That's roughly the length and width of a football field on both sides. The hole appeared in 1972 when the roof of an underground aquifer collapsed. Neighbors said they heard the sound of trees crashing in the middle of the night and the sinkhole was discovered a few days later from people hunting in the woods. The sinkhole was named "Golly Hole" based on the expressions and reactions of those who stumbled upon it initially.[7]

Sinkholes can be very damaging and destructive. They appear suddenly, and in places you would have never guessed. The size of the sinkhole is difficult to determine, as much of what is happening is underground. The Golly Hole is said to have been caused by a drought that dried up the water table underneath, leaving a large cavity with no support. Though sinkholes are scary and can cause great damage, they can also leave behind some of the most beautiful watering holes and scenery on earth.

No one stays at their job forever. At some point, you will leave your current position. It may be due to layoffs, budget cuts, or a restructure, or it may be a part-time position with a timeline and end date. Perhaps you were not retained due to a new vision or new leadership. Regardless of the reason, it is worth asking what kind of hole you will leave behind you. To borrow from the sinkhole analogy, imagine taking your hand and placing it in a bucket of water. When you pull your hand back out, notice how fast the water fills in. You cannot stop physics.

When you leave, your job will be filled. You cannot control that. What size hole can you leave behind? How you do your job, the relational deposits you make, the new systems you build, and the growth or increase you generate will be seen once you leave. Will it be small, insignificant, and unnoticed or will it be like the Golly Hole, deep and wide?

Let's look at five different ways you can leave a "big hole" behind when your time comes to transition.

1. **Invest in Relationships** – our job as leaders is to relate to others. Our success or failure stands on this one factor. Our ability to operate within small communities of various kinds of people can create lasting impact or leave us feeling unimportant and undervalued. Like destructive sinkholes we can leave a job feeling empty and hollow if we are not able to invest and build with others relationally. With the ever-increasing access to online training, the need to relate well with others and operate with a high level of social intelligence will be crucial skills for recruiters.. Skills like carrying on a casual conversation, listening without distraction, maintaining eye contact, and showing interest in what others are saying will be skills that set candidates apart. The frequency and ratio of interacting with others face-to-face rather than online or over text is heavily lopsided.

Failure to use a certain skill causes that skill level to diminish. If you are not skilled at something as simple as relating to others it will be clumsy and odd at first. However, the more you do it, the better you will become at it. Leaving a big hole behind will come down to your ability to invest in relationships at work.

2. **Competence With Technology** – learn how to use new technology. You might be saying, " Didn't you just say to invest in relationships not online?" I did but, with today's trends in performance, it is imperative we get comfortable using new technologies. We are living in a time where every single thing we do can be quantified and measured with technology. In my role, we place GPS units on each athlete to measure the amounts of stress on the body during practice, use force plate testing weekly to track jumping and landing trends over the course of a season, and do DEXA scans to look at body compositions and bone densities. The list is endless and not all are necessary. However, minimally you will need to understand how technology works, how to integrate changes in your plan from the data, and continue learning as you go. This has changed drastically from when I first started out. Using technology is the new norm and it is not going away anytime soon.

Practically speaking, older and more seasoned leaders will typically need to spend more time online to learn how to capture, read and provide detailed reports with all of the various technologies. While these leaders may be great at personally relating to others, there is often the need to spend some time learning how to utilize and implement more technology. Similarly, younger coaches may be more comfortable online than in in-person interactions, so their focus should be spent improving in-person interactions and perfecting their soft-skills. Seeking to strike a balance between the role you are working in and the key responsibilities you carry, will be imperative for increasing your personal impact on others. Younger employees who cannot relate, run the risk of people not knowing who they are or what they do because they are always on the computer and never speak up. Older seasoned staff run the risk of becoming obsolete or outdated if they cannot be open to learning new skills or at least have someone who can help them with those deficiencies.

3. **Assisting Other Staff** – when it comes to being in an orchestra, no one likes playing second fiddle. Almost everyone wants to be in the lead. When it comes to leaving a big hole behind with your job, assisting and serving others is high up on the chart for making a big impact. Though you are not out front leading and directing, you can still have great influence behind the scenes. In fact, I have found a lot of people flourish in these types of behind the scenes roles. For years and years, this was a role I filled and still do currently at times. There are benefits to being an assistant that can be very rewarding especially if those you are working alongside value, appreciate, and respect the work you are doing. To help illustrate this point, I love the poem by Ella Wheeler Wilcox entitled "Two Kinds of People."[8] There are two main types of people in the world. Those who lift and those who lean. Lifter's make everyone's job a little easier. Leaner's make your job more difficult and stringent. Take a closer look at the poem for more insight:

Two Kinds of People
by Ella Wheeler Wilcox

There are two kinds of people on earth today,
Two kinds of people, no more, I say.
Not the good or the bad, for 'tis well understood,
The good are half bad and the bad are half good.

Not the happy and sad, for the swift-flying years
Bring each man his laughter and each man his tears.
Not the rich and the poor, for to count a man's wealth
You must first know the state of his conscience and health.

Not the humble and proud, for in life's busy span
Who puts on vain airs is not counted as a man.
No! The two kinds of people on earth I mean
Are the people who lift, and the people who lean.

Wherever you go you will find the world's masses
Are ever divided into these two classes.
And, strangely enough, you will find, too, I wean,
There is only one lifter to twenty who lean.

This one question I ask. Are you easing the load
Of overtaxed lifters who toil down the road?
Or are you a leaner who lets others bear
Your portion of worry and labor and care?

The main question you will need to ask yourself is this: Do I make the person's job I am assisting with easier? Can they feel the 'lift' of weight of responsibility they are carrying because you make it easier? Are those you are working with having to work harder now because you don't follow through on tasks or you lack taking initiative and need more oversight to stay motivated? If you are going to leave a big hole behind, be a 'lifter' and assist others well.

4. **Develop Your Superpower** – I love superhero movies. The one thing I love about them is everyone on the team has a superpower that is unique and different than everyone else's. Each super hero uses their special power to help the team win and defeat the bad guys. In a similar way, every staff is a team of unique individuals

with certain skill sets. If you want to leave a big hole, find a talent or gift you are really good at and develop it. Everyone cannot be great at everything. In today's performance economy, it's all about placing a performance team around each athlete to help them be successful. Having a skill that no one else has or becoming the local expert on a topic, piece of equipment, or training system will increase the value you bring to the table. You can literally be the "go to" person for whatever that might be. In my profession, specialties like speed work, excel spreadsheets, program design, internships, content development, specialized certifications or organizational skills are just a few areas where an individual can strengthen a performance team. Look for an area you not only are passionate about but also something you are really good at. Passion will not be enough to get you by. You will need to be competent and skilled in an area that adds value to the performance team.

5. **Have a "Legacy" Mindset** – successful leaders always leave a legacy. Great leaders build something big enough that it lives beyond them. Martin Luther King Jr. is a leader who I have studied for years and even today he continues to impact lives for the better. Though we may never attain the level of influence and notoriety of Dr. King, we can still have a motive and goal of building something big enough that those who come behind you benefit from it. It could be something as simple as building enough trust and credibility that the role you have as a voluntary intern gets turned into a part-time position with more responsibility. When the day comes and you move on, the person behind you will benefit greatly. Their lives will be better because of your hard work. That is leaving a bigger hole behind. Another way you may do this is repairing a strained relationship history from the previous staff member in your role. It may take years to repair the trust and rapport but doing so demonstrates a "legacy"

mindset. Doing your job in such a way that it's not only for you. You are performing your job to benefit and help others. You are not just looking out for yourself. You have a big picture view of your career and truly care about how it impacts others.

Take a moment and reflect. Here are some questions to ask yourself for application: If you were to miss a day of work and not show up, would anyone notice? Would your co-workers ask where you are that day? Would other people notice? Additionally, what if you were taken off working with a certain task or project? Would those who work alongside you be saddened or would they be relieved? These questions will be critical for you to answer or find out what kind of impact you are currently having. When the day comes to leave your position, will your "sink hole" be small, metaphorically speaking, without anyone ever noticing? Or, will it be like the Golly Hole in Alabama? So big that bystanders who see it are astounded at the size of it. As you continue to pursue your leadership goals and grow as a leader, strive to leave a big hole behind you. In doing so, you will not only be rewarded but also respected over time as you advance in your career path.

CHAPTER 3

PROFESSIONALISM

*"Professional is not a label you give yourself,
it's a description you hope others will apply to you."*

—

DAVID MAISTER

Got Professionalism?

I hate wearing suits and getting dressed up. One of my favorite perks of being an athlete was lounging around in my shorts and t-shirts. In my senior year I had to sit for my senior pictures. You know the ones: cheesy backgrounds and heavily posed photos you cringe at when you are older. I did not own a tie or a jacket, so my Dad dragged me to the store and bought a jacket for my pictures. I was smiling in my pictures, but inside I felt like a caged animal, desperate to be free from the confines of a constricted outfit. I still don't enjoy dressing up, but I have realized the importance of putting your best foot forward.

Professionalism is important.. Professional, as defined by Merriam-Webster, means : *"exhibiting a courteous, conscientious, and generally businesslike manner in the workplace."*[9] As an intern, I had not heard of the word *professional*. I loved coaching because I loved to train and it was a perk not to have to wear a suit and tie every day. As I was promoted and managed more responsibilities, it became very clear to me that some of my personal habits were not very professional. When my mentor pulled me aside and told me I needed to start shaving more regularly, I knew he was right. If I was tired or busy, I had a habit of letting my facial hair go for too long and it was a bad look.

As a leader, how you present yourself to others can cause some perception problems. The clothes we wear, our grooming habits, and how we walk and talk all send a clear message about our professionalism. The more professional we are, the more serious others will take us. If you want to advance in your career and stand out, you must raise the bar on your physical appearance. Imagine getting on a plane and the pilot isn't wearing a formal uniform. He has his beard grown out and is dipping tobacco with his feet kicked up on the dash of the plane, all while speaking profanities to the flight attendants. Would you feel good about your flight? Would you want to stay on? Would you continue flying with that airline? What about investing your money? Imagine the owner of the bank was a woman with unkempt hair, who showed up late wearing jeans and a dirty tee shirt, had a scowl on her face, and did not pay attention while you were talking about the large amounts of money you planned to invest? Would you feel inclined to trust her with your hard-earned money?

When you are a leader in the working world, the level of trust, respect, credibility and admiration you get from the team of professionals you work with, will have a direct impact on the level of success you have. Not only that, it will also work to either strengthen or weaken the relationships you have with the clients you serve and work with on a daily basis. If you really want to lead one day, it's time to start acting like it. A lot of people might say, I will act like it when I get the position. No you won't. That's not how it works. In John Maxwell's book the *360 Degree*

Leader, he addresses this issue and refers to it as "The Position Myth."[10] The position myth states, 'When I get the position then I will become a leader'. That is incorrect. You will get the position when you become a leader. The key to career advancement is positioning yourself as a leader to earn the position you want. Dress and act like the leader you want to be one day. When you do, you will not only be perceived differently, you will work with a higher level of excellence in everything you do.

Years ago, I had a desperately needed wakeup call in the area of professionalism. A very famous track athlete was opening a performance facility nearby. He visited campus, and spent most of the day talking with my boss and checking out our facilities for input and insight. When my boss brought our guest to meet me, I was down on the floor working with some athletes. I was in a good mood and acting silly during the session, which I often did if the vibes were good. As my boss introduced me to our guest, I continued in my silly demeanor and didn't think anything of it. Later, my boss pulled me aside and said, "I know you were having a good time coaching and being yourself, but you have to be aware of how you are coming off to others." He went on to say, "If you want to lead one day, you must learn to carry yourself better." That hurt to hear, but I realized he was right and I have never forgotten that advice.

Lack of professionalism can hold you back. I have seen it happen with young professionals as well as seasoned veterans. Their career momentum is hindered because they lack professionalism in one or more areas of their lives. In my line of work, you can have all the book smarts in the world. You can be knowledgeable in biomechanics, physiology, periodization, program design, nutrition, and running mechanics, but if you cannot present yourself with excellence as a coach, you will not be taken very seriously. Let's look at five areas you can come up higher in as you strive to improve your professionalism.

1. Appearance – your dress attire sends a message before you ever open your mouth. Your hairstyle, clothes, and personal hygiene, seem like small things, but they contribute to the message you are sending about yourself. If you don't care how you look others may wonder what other areas of your life are not well cared for. When others see you in a positive light, they expect more from you and your professionalism carries over into other aspects of your job.

2. **Attitude** – it is your professional responsibility to show up at work consistently in a good mood. In many ways, your attitude is like a paintbrush and the work you do is your canvas. If you go around everyday "painting" or "spraying" all the projects and people you work on with a bad, sour, grumpy attitude no one will want to work with you or be around you. Not only that, the quality of your work will not be your very best. In all my years in leading and serving others, I have rarely seen someone with a bad attitude at work avoid the negative consequences of that in their work and relationships. Think about it. When you talk with someone over the phone at a business, you can hear them smile. What is that? It's their attitude coming through. They are in a good mood, pleasant to talk with, and helpful. It is subtle, but it makes a difference. Your attitude can set you apart as a professional. Our tone of voice has energy in it: positive or negative. The words we use can either draw others to us, or repel them. Someone who is negative, complaining all the time, or sour about life can be a drag to be around. Leading can be hard at times, but a big part of being a professional is not bringing your personal life or feelings into your job every day. Separate your personal life from your work life. Using bad language, cursing, or inappropriate jokes can hurt your reputation. I have seen poor language habits keep someone from getting a job or receiving a promotion. There may be times you need to get emotional and use some stronger language, I have witnessed it used in a purposeful manner where

it yielded positive results. However, as a rule, you should strive to be cognizant of what words you use, how often you use them as well as the emotion behind them. The best leaders do not have to curse or be negative to motivate someone. A professional will strive to be an effective communicator by choosing language and tone suitable to the situation.

3. **Organization** – the more organized you are the more comfortable others will be working with you. The cleanliness of your car, office space, break room, calendar, staff, and how you run meetings or events let others know how much you care about your job. When you take pride in your work, it shows. Additionally, being organized allows you to be more efficient and effective with your time and space. You will get more done and things will run more smoothly. Disorganization sends the message you are winging it: 'I didn't put much time into this because it doesn't matter much to me'. If your office is in disarray, people might think 'What a messy person… If this is messy, what else in their lives is a mess?' Appearing unorganized can oftentimes reduce the confidence others might have in you.

4. **Courteous** – saying please and thank you goes a long way. You catch more flies with honey than vinegar. As a leader, there will be times you need to be demanding and driven to get results. That is what leaders do, they make things happen. As you do, don't forget to be polite and courteous. Show appreciation to those you oversee. The best leaders lead with both passion and compassion, not either or. If all you have is passion, you run the risk of becoming a tyrant and running people into the ground. On the other hand, if all you have is compassion and no drive, you can get taken advantage of and be perceived as a pushover. You can be the velvet hammer. You get results,

make things happen, but you are pleasant to work with. Being courteous about the little things goes a long way when leading.

5. **Business Ethics** – how you treat others and how you make decisions boil down to one thing: core values. Don't listen to what people say, watch what they do. I have heard leaders talking about their team as family, but turn around and treat them with disrespect. They gossip and talk bad about them behind their backs. They make dishonest or shady decisions or they talk to them in a way that devalues them. If you really want to see the core values of a leader, watch how they treat someone who cannot do anything to help them. I have had the privilege of working with some world class professionals and the best ones treat others with respect regardless of title, position, or salary. Leadership is stewardship: nobody owes you anything. You must earn people's trust and respect. Leaders exist to serve and help others, to build others up. By treating others this way and serving them, you become great in their eyes and they will want to follow you. In John Maxwell's book *"Winning With People"*[11] he talks about three different roads we can take in how we treat others:

   A. **The Low Road** – You treat others worse than they deserve to be treated.

   B. **The Middle Road** – You treat others exactly how they deserve to be treated.

   C. **The High Road** – You treat others better than they deserve to be treated.

In all my years as a coach and a professional, I have never seen someone regret taking the high road. At the end of the day, being a leader is all about being the bigger person. Anytime you stoop down to hurt someone or make them feel small, you lower yourself to that level as well. It's never worth it. Grow up and stand up professionally. It will serve you well for years to come.

Remember the milk commercial with the tagline "Got Milk"? Whenever someone was drinking milk, they were left with a white milk mustache. You could see it. Playing on the classic childhood milk mustache, the commercial illustrated the importance of drinking milk as adults. Though the evidence of your leadership may not be a white milk mustache, your lack of professionalism will show. Level up in your professionalism. Dress sharp, communicate with clean language, tighten up your digital presence, get organized and most of all treat others with respect no matter what role they (or you) play. Though you may not have a milk mustache, people will know you "Got Professionalism".

Personal Branding

In 8th grade, all I wanted was a Members Only jacket. All the cool kids were wearing one and if you didn't have one, you were left out of the group. When my mom bought the one I wanted, I could not wait to wear it to school. I was so sure I would be viewed and treated differently. I would be accepted and welcomed into the cool kids club. I wore that jacket every day for weeks, and may have even slept in it. Even in one hundred degree heat I wasn't taking it off.

Occasionally, I would spill something on the jacket while I was eating. When this happened, I would panic and dive into emergency cleaning mode. I became so good at getting the most stubborn and odd stains out of that material I could have opened my own dry cleaning service. That Members Only jacket was a brand for me, and it was life. It gave me confidence, joy and self-assurance around my peers. It influenced that year for me as a young teenager. Receiving recognition, acceptance and getting noticed by others who normally wouldn't notice you, has a profound impact on a young person. That is the power of a brand.

Branding today has changed quite a bit but its power and impact continue to be far-reaching. Certain brands gain more social recognition and improve how others perceive you. Whether it is the product, or the company behind it, branding matters. Today, branding does not solely rest in the hands of the seller. Back then, you had to buy the product, wear the apparel, drive the car, or join the club to gain influence and change perception. Today we have the power to brand ourselves and shape how we are perceived. Social media has been a major player in allowing this to take place. If you are serious about moving up in your career and becoming an excellent professional, you will need to embrace the principles and power of personal branding.

When talking about branding, there are two main buckets to focus on: Internal branding and external branding. External branding forms what others think of you. Impressions about your external branding begin with whatever they can find about you on the internet. With internal branding, it's all about who you really are. Those you work the closest with and have daily interactions with have formed opinions about you whether you are aware of their opinions or not. This section will focus primarily on internal branding. Though external branding is important, I have found the most important to be the internal piece. Those who work directly with you and know you the best are the most powerful when leading. As you move up and gain years of experience, your external brand will become more needed. For now, let's look closer at the internal, or personal, branding of your job.

To start with, let's define personal branding. According to Wikipedia, "Personal branding is the conscious and intentional effort to create and influence public perception of an individual by positioning them as an authority in their industry, elevating their credibility, and differentiating themselves from the competition, to ultimately advance their career, increase their circle of influence, and have a larger impact."[12] I love this definition because most people do not realize how they are perceived, especially younger coaches. How they think others see them and how others really see them are totally different. This is crucially important as a professional because if you don't know how you are coming off to others, you will hit roadblocks and barriers in your career and will be frustrated on why you cannot seem to move up. The problem with this is simple. Most of us don't put much thought into our personal brand. We are who we are. I am not suggesting you be fake. By no means. Authenticity rules in today's leadership economy. However, I am saying it is very important for you to not only know what your personal brand is but also how you are being perceived. These two facets will have large implications on what ceiling you set for yourself as you pursue bigger career goals.

When I first heard the topic of personal branding and how important it was, it really helped me understand why I had struggled in different areas of my career and why others I knew were having a hard time. I understand as I am writing this some people could care less what others think of them and how they are perceived. There is some truth in that. You need to be secure and know who you are. You don't want to be a chameleon and change every time someone doesn't like you or something you did. I'm not talking about that. What I am saying is, if you really want to prepare and position yourself for leadership, you must purposely and intentionally start thinking about your personal brand and begin shaping it. You have the power and control to paint a picture of what your brand is with everyone you come in contact with. Building your personal brand works just the same as it does with a product or a business. You do it one person at a time. The more interactions you have with others around you over a period of time, the more your brand becomes known and set. The longer you work somewhere, the harder it becomes to change your brand. It is doable, but will take more effort. Once your brand has been built, that is who you are. It can help or hurt you depending on what it is.

To help you understand this concept, I recommend a simple exercise to try with those you work closest with. You can either email them, meet with them individually, or send out a survey to gather the information.

You will need to think through how you do this to ensure you get the most accurate and honest feedback possible. Ask each person to write down three words to describe what it is like working with you. It should be no more than three words. Less is better so you can form a clear picture. Once you do this exercise, you might be surprised by what others say, either positive or negative. After you do this, ask yourself if this is how you wanted to be portrayed by others? Is it accurate? The power of this little exercise does wonders for you. First, it gets you thinking about the impression you give others. Second, it sends a message to your co-workers that you are willing to improve, and you care about the work you do. Lastly, it will open you up to the idea of how you can start working to improve your brand. Though you are not Nike, Apple, or Disney, you are very unique in your own way and your personal brand can set you apart from others in your industry and that will make the difference. Let's look at five aspects you should consider when building your personal brand no matter where you work or what position you hold.

1. **First Impressions** – when someone meets you for the first time you have a very unique opportunity to set yourself up for success or failure. This initial interaction can leave a good or bad taste in someone's mouth. Are you over-the-top and outgoing, or are you timid, withdrawn and quiet? It's kind of like dating. You both are feeling each other out at first, forming judgements, perceptions and thoughts on whether you like the other or want to work with them or not. One of the principles I have learned to go by when first meeting someone for the first time is being interested versus being interesting. You want to engage with them, show interest in them, and demonstrate that you want to get to know them better. In doing so, you will disarm them and send a message that you care about people. They will walk away from your time together with a positive feeling about the exchange and will most likely look forward to interacting again. Emotions can be very powerful in forming

perceptions, especially with first impressions. Being a genuinely curious person that is interested in others will take you a long way. The saying of "You never get a second chance to make a first impression" is very true.

2. **Buttoned Up** – think about all the best companies or stores you shop at. You probably don't always pay attention, but most companies have their employees dress a certain way. If they dress nicely, you won't always notice. If their attire is sloppy or unkempt you will notice right away, and that impression can influence how often you shop there. Take for example, military personnel. They are "buttoned up". Their hat is on straight, clothes pressed, buttons and belt buckled lined up and polished, pants pleated, and shoes shining. They are dressed to impress. I am not saying you need to look militant, but raising your standard of excellence in what you wear can have a profound impact on your personal brand. Not only will you get noticed and stand out as a leader, you will carry yourself with more confidence and raise the level of your work.

3. **Enjoyable to Work With** – ninety-nine percent of the time people want to work with those they enjoy working with. Inevitably, we will also have to work with those they don't like to, but our default is to be drawn to those who are pleasant to work with. In the long run, if you are very difficult to work with, it can damage your reputation and hinder career advancement. To be clear here, I am not talking about being a pushover. Being too aggressive and combative is an extreme, as is being a pushover and people-pleaser. Neither extreme suits a leader. With one, people don't want to be around you and with the other, you have trouble garnering respect and maintaining credibility.

Be the person people enjoy working with. Be approachable. Every person has one of two faces on them at all times. A "yes" face or a "no" face. Which one are you? Being approachable sends the message that you are open to dialogue and interaction. If you are hard to read and people don't feel like they can come to you, they will eventually shy away from working with you. Being approachable means you are not moody or unstable emotionally. If you are grumpy for no apparent reason and fly off the handle at any moment, others will walk on eggshells around you and find you exhausting. Being consistently in a good mood and checking your emotions when something is bothering you is key. This will go a long way in building your brand.

4. **Reliability** – any successful brand in business has one thing that has kept them in the game: reliability. Being reliable seems simple and insignificant but if you are not reliable you are not delivering. Every single person we work with has expectations of us. Not understanding those expectations and not meeting them will significantly damage your personal brand. You cannot do everything, of course, and you will either need to communicate your limitations or learn to delegate aspects of your job to get it done. If you don't delegate, you can become overwhelmed and unreliable, causing you to miss deadlines, turn in half-completed work, or do a half-hearted job. Being reliable isn't just showing up; it involves doing everything with excellence and high standards. Being reliable over time will pay huge dividends in building your personal brand.

5. **Ratings and Reviews** – you can rate and review everything today. With the click of a button, you can access other people's opinions and experiences on any product or company. These reviews can have a profound effect on buyers, especially if you are torn between which product to use. Naturally, you will go with the product or person that has a strong track record of doing a great job. In leadership

it pays to be aware that your coworkers talk to each other. Guess what they talk about to others after they have worked with you for a while? You. What it was like working with or for you. Though they are not leaving written reviews or following a five star rating system, what they are saying makes a difference to your personal brand.

How you treat others and how you make them feel is like writing on their hearts. The memories built by your interactions with others reach far beyond those you know. Stories about you will also reach those you don't know. Questions like: What is 'so and so' like to work with? What kind of person are they? Do they know their stuff? These, plus many other questions, can lead to conversations that are similar to ratings and reviews that add positive or negative weight to your personal brand.

In summary, as professionals we have to put careful thought into our personal brand. This is not quick or easy, but it is worth doing. It may make you uncomfortable, or you may think it doesn't concern you, but at some point you must address it. You are the owner of your brand. If you don't realize this and take ownership, someone else will do it for you. You work too hard, and it's too competitive in today's job market not to use it for your benefit. Just like my Members Only jacket gave me a small advantage with my friends and social circle in the 8th grade, so today intentionally building your personal brand will end up being the edge you need to get the position. Be aware every day that your brand is showing! Make sure it's the one you want.

The Digital Handshake

We sat in the room as a staff and whittled down the job applicant pool to several finalists. We were leaning heavily towards one candidate in particular. His resume looked great, he had plenty of experience, his references were solid and we were about to call and invite him in for an in-person interview. There was one last thing I saw that changed my mind. The letter of interest was addressed to the wrong person and place. Most likely, the applicant was sending out letters to multiple job openings and didn't double check his work. It cost him an invitation. Though we didn't know the applicant at all, this was an oversight that caused us to pause. The nature of the job he applied for would require attention to detail and right here in the initial stages of introducing himself, his digital handshake did not leave a good impression. If he missed such a small detail on his application, what else would he miss if he had the job? These are little things but they are big things that separate candidates for interviews or not.

Your online presence impacts your professionalism. In the same way you leave an impression when you shake hands with someone in person, how you appear when someone sees you or interacts with you online is your digital handshake. It is a first impression that can help or hinder you. Everyone and everything you want to find about a person is online. Resumes are still used but they are more of a formality than anything else. If you have never done a Google search on your name, I highly recommend trying it. Not only do it once but check it several times a year. You will be surprised by what comes up. The first two pages of the search are who you are, whether you like it or not. Those of you who dislike social media and say it doesn't matter to you, listen up. As Cal Newport says, be a digital minimalist.[13] What I mean by that is, don't use online platforms or social media for over-indulgence, addiction, and distraction; use it as a tool to leverage your career. Social media and online networking sites like LinkedIn can be powerful tools that allow you to brand yourself and tell a narrative of who you are and what you do. Tools like these can help set you apart more than any other time in the history of the world. It *does* matter and it *does* make a difference. Let's look at five ways to "level up" your digital handshake as a leader:

1. **Social Media** – what platforms do you currently use? What kind of photos have you posted? Who do you follow and what are your interests? Do you post content regularly? Is it educational or entertaining? Does your content inspire or embarrass? What would your peers say about your content? Have you posted anything questionable or inappropriate? How many selfies do you have? These are questions for an initial inventory to assess your digital handshake. Keep in mind, the greater the visibility and influence you have as a leader the more you will be scrutinized and judged.

2. **Email** – if someone were to read your emails, what would they say about you as a professional? Do you speak in clear sentences? What about punctuation and grammar? Do you proofread before you hit "send"? Do you send scathing, angry emails? Have you ever said anything inappropriate over email? One thing you must take into account is any email you send is either stored in a cloud or someone else has it on their computer. Once online, always online! Though it may seem insignificant, your emails tell people a lot about you.. Act accordingly.

3. **Texting** – how do you talk over text? This may seem way too personal but this is the world we live in. Nothing is hidden these days. Everything you send over text can be screenshotted, stored, sent, and saved. I have seen this play out for someone not getting a job: the words this individual texted became a roadblock to his application. Texting should be for communication to inform or confirm. Anything serious or confrontational should be addressed in person. Too much can be taken out of context via text messages. The dangers of living in a digital world is an increasing avoidance of hard, uncomfortable conversations in person. Texting someone with the risks of being misconstrued, misunderstood, or misinterpreted is not worth it. Raising your professionalism over text is a must. I saw

a situation one time, where a certain employee left his phone out and people walking by could see his text messages. He was complaining about his job and how unhappy he was in one of the texts. His boss ended up walking by and seeing it. Not only did it cause a strain on his relationship with his boss, it hurt him professionally. While it wasn't appropriate for the boss to see the text, it did happen. Tighten up your text and safeguard your career.

4. **Videos/Online Meetings** – if we learned anything from the COVID-19 pandemic, video or Zoom meetings matter. Not being in person should not affect your level of excellence. How you show up in an online meeting can change or damage your professional image. I recall when we were in lock down at the start of the pandemic, some people would have cats walking across the screen during a serious meeting. Another person's bed would be a mess in the background, or they would look like they crawled out from under the bed right before we started. Some people would lie down during the meeting or never turn their screen. They were too relaxed and let their guard down, sending a bad message and completely changing how that individual was viewed. If you have a lot of online meetings, step up your game. Show up online the way you would in person.

5. **Podcasts, Portfolios, and Projects** – when was the last time you did a project and posted it online? It could be a white paper, a LinkedIn post, a vlog, or a new website. There are so many different ways to improve your digital handshake online. You would be shocked at how doing one small thing with excellence captures the attention of someone you have never met. A short podcast interview can introduce you to hundreds of people you would never meet in person. You never know when that one person you had a positive impact on from something you posted will aid you in your career as a leader.

Your digital handshake carries weight. Do your due diligence to ensure your online presence is an asset and not a liability. If you are serious about your digital handshake, have a trusted colleague or a hiring manager do an evaluation of your online presence. Ask them to grade you on these criteria:

- Consistency across multiple platforms (professional photos, titles, and images).
- The language and content of your emails and texts.
- Is there anything inappropriate or unprofessional posted on your social media accounts?
- Videos, website, podcasts, white papers, or projects (your portfolio).

As you think about your digital handshake, don't just go and do everything everyone else is doing. You will get far more return off doing something clean, sharp, and simple that matches who you are as a professional than doing too much. Reflect and think about some of the people you have met in person as a professional over the years. What did they do that stood out to you and impressed you? Those can be little clues and hints to what matters to you most when meeting someone in person. In a similar way, take that same approach to how you introduce yourself online. Take it seriously and pay attention to details just like you would when introducing yourself in person. Keep it simple, be excellent, and make a great first impression. It may end up being the difference maker that gives you an edge over the competition and lands you the job.

CHAPTER 4

AUTHENTICITY

"You were born an original, don't die a copy."

—

JOHN MASON

Taking the Armor Off – The Power of Authenticity

Authenticity is a critical component for your success as a leader. We live in an age where people can act one way in one group and portray themselves as someone totally different in another setting. Like a chameleon, they change colors depending on who they are with. If you happen to see them in both groups, it can lead to confusion about who they really are. They are posers and pretenders. Fakes may work for a while, but eventually they are found out. A strong synonym for authenticity is the word *sincere*. The Latin root of *sincere* divides the word into two parts: *sin* meaning "without", and *ceras* meaning "wax."[14] Dishonest Roman or Greek sculptors would frequently cover flaws in their work with wax in order to deceive a viewer or buyer. According to tradition, if an artist did not cover their work with wax, it was viewed as a mark of authenticity. Being sincere literally meant "without wax". Authentic leadership demands the same authenticity. No one is expecting perfection, but you need to keep it real. Insincerity risks lowering the value, worth and respect you need to make a lasting impact.

When I started taking on more visible roles with more influence early on in my coaching career, there was pressure to act a certain way." *You have to be tough; you have to be a hardass and carry yourself more like a militant leader".* At first, I caved in and worked so hard at being a tough guy. It was exhausting, I wasn't happy, and no one was buying it. I eventually realized I couldn't sustain it. I removed the tough guy armor and decided to do "me", no matter how good or bad it was. If nobody liked my style of leadership, that was fine. I would rather be authentic than keep changing and be miserable. You can only succeed in life by being yourself. Changing who you are and copying someone else's style of leadership may work for awhile, but eventually it will catch up to you. Take off your armor and be the very best version of you! Let's look at five powerful reasons to embrace authenticity and stay true to yourself.

1. **It's Attractive** – there is nothing more attractive than an authentic leader. When you meet an authentic leader, you want to spend time with them. You want to follow them and get on board with their vision. Leadership is about getting others to buy in and take action. When you are real and authentic, others naturally get on board and follow. Having people bought in because of your authenticity is much more effective and long lasting than "waxing over" your behaviors all the time and deceiving people.

2. **It's Credible** – credibility is a passport for leadership. Authentic leaders have a way of selling who they are and why you should believe in them. There is no pretense or putting on a show. Authentic leadership is consistent and real. They are comfortable in their own skin whether you like it or not. An authentic leader is credible.

3. **It's Vulnerable** – a vulnerable leader is unafraid to be human. When a leader is authentic, their vulnerability garners respect. They hold themselves to a high standard, but aren't afraid to admit their mistakes. They are approachable and understand we all struggle and fail at times. Just as the ancient sculptors' artwork was more valuable when they didn't cover up the imperfections of their work, your leadership will have more impact by being vulnerable at times. This is where the art of leadership comes in. Knowing when, where, and how to be vulnerable. The timing and context will need to be considered. Being vulnerable at the right time, at the right place, and with the right people can make a difference and increase your impact.

4. **It's Refreshing** – authentic leadership is refreshing. Leaders who are insincere or constantly playing political games can wear you out. Authentic leaders will see you for who you are and empower you to be you. Being able to be yourself not only refreshes you, but allows you to flourish in your strengths. Authentic leaders seek your sincerity as much as you seek theirs.

5. **It's Lasting** – the best leaders have lasting impact. If you are fake and ingenuine you may be able to get away with it for a while but the deception will not last. I have tried this myself and failed miserably. Charisma is powerful and persuasive but authenticity ensures for the long haul. There is no hidden agenda, no games, no pretense. Goals and missions are articulated and communicated for the benefit of everyone.

CHAPTER 5

COMPETENCE

"To be a manager requires more than a title, a big office and other outward symbols of rank. It requires competence and performance of a high order."

—

PETER DRUCKER

You're In Charge. Now What?

It's happened. The promotion you have been working for, waiting for, and preparing for is yours. Your ship has finally come in. Your time is here. You have the title, position, and office you have been dreaming of. The new business cards have arrived and the excitement and energy from your friends and family is intoxicating. It's almost a little funny when the moment finally comes. Often, it will come when you least expect it and in ways you could never think or dream of. You never really are fully ready for that promotion. Getting promoted to leadership positions is very similar to how they train pilots to fly planes. Pilots spend a certain number of hours in a flight simulator before they can fly a real plane. Flying a virtual plane in a simulator is great and all, but if you crash the plane, you just hit the reset button and try again. Nobody gets injured or dies. You keep practicing until you figure it out. However, no matter how good you get at the flight simulator, you must fly a real plane in the real sky before you are qualified and certified to fly, take real lives on board and keep them safe. Leadership can be very similar. Everything you do until you get that first promotion is practice for the real thing. You make mistakes that you and others don't always feel. You learn from mistakes, grow from them, and keep practicing and practicing. Until the day comes you get promoted.

You are in charge, now what? What are you going to do? It's your turn to fly the plane with real people on board. Mistakes at this point are costly. People can get hurt and there is no reset button. Your actions, attitudes, decision-making ability, communication style, people skills, and professionalism will be on full display. It will not just be tested; it will be exposed for what it really is. If there is one thing, getting promoted will lead to more pressure. Pressure magnifies. If you have problems with pride and insecurity, it will be evident. Your struggle with anger and lack of self-control will erupt when someone hits your hot button. Your tendency towards being a workaholic and burnout will have a new open field to play in. Promotions have such an outward appeal and appearance of glamor, admiration, and adulation and it does, for a moment. There is nothing like it. It is worth every ounce of effort and sacrifice you put into it. But at the end of the day, you're in charge. As the leader, what do you do? <u>Let's look at five things you can do once you are in charge to start you off on the right foot.</u>

1. **Have a 90-day Plan** – getting promoted will be overwhelming the first time it happens. You will go from following to leading. The pressure you will feel and receive from your new position will be weighty. You will inherit problems you have never had, lead people you do not know, and gain new enemies you never knew existed.

With that being said, I would strongly recommend not thinking too far in the future at first. What do you want to focus your time and energies on for the first 90 days? Write down the problems and pressures you are currently facing. Prioritize them in order of urgency. What are the top one or two things you can develop a plan of attack for? Do you need to evaluate your staff? Do you need to make budget cuts? Do you need to reorganize as a whole? Are other departments or staff outside your area disgruntled with you? Do you have a branding and image problem? Whatever the issue is, sit down, draw up a 90-day plan and lay out the execution steps. List the key stakeholders you will need to meet and communicate with before you move forward. You don't need to give them all the details necessarily, but they do need to know the new direction. Remember, people are always 'down' on what they are not 'up' on. In other words, most people don't like surprises when it comes to hearing information for the first time in a meeting or public arena, especially when it involves them. Be proactive in your communication when planning and making changes. Talking about plans you have in advance allows people to process information, ask questions and provide feedback. The more you involve others in the process, the better buy-in from them at the start.

2. **Plan a Site Visit** – go visit someone who has been leading longer than you. You would be surprised how much wisdom and inspiration you can glean from someone more accomplished than you. Make a list of questions you want to ask them. How do they lead their staff? How do they organize their time and resources? What are their biggest mistakes they have made? What would they do differently if they had to start all over again? How do they manage up? How do they keep a good work-life balance? When you first get

promoted, you are like a fresh piece of clay. Getting input and learning from seasoned leaders will help shape how you lead early on.

3. **Plan a Regular Diet of Consuming Content on Leadership** – if you want to lead and lead well, you must continuously learn. Leaders are learners, and learners are leaders. The two go hand in hand. If you aren't learning, you aren't leading. Plain and simple. Find the top podcasts, videos, books, and seminars on how to lead at a higher level. You will unlock problems, gain new perspectives, receive fresh insights on how to look at situations, and find endless inspiration to keep rising to new levels as a leader. You won't be able to do it all the time, but if you make it a lifelong habit, it will pay dividends in your career.

4. **Find Your Wingman** – When you step at the helm to lead, the first thing you will find out fast is you cannot do it alone. You must have someone you can trust and lean on. Find your wingman. Find someone loyal who is dependable and trustworthy. They will push back if they think you can do better, but they will also give you a heads up if something isn't right in an area you may not see clearly. A wingman gives you a sense of peace and confidence you wouldn't otherwise have. They will cover your weaknesses, balance your strengths, and help guide you when making hard decisions. They will have your back. If you don't have someone like this when you get promoted, you will need to make this a priority to find one or hire one. Don't stop until you get it done.

5. **Get Clarity on What You Will Be Evaluated On** – how will you be evaluated? Who will have a voice in it? What areas will be weighing in on how you did? Is it one-person, multiple persons, or multiple departments? Who can you not afford to make angry? Who do you need to pay special attention to and check in with regularly? Will

you be evaluated with a numerical grid, or just a written evaluation? I have had different types of evaluations over the years, and ultimately, it really helps to know what targets you should be aiming at before you start throwing darts. You can come up with a great plan, but if in that plan you don't have a key area or key performance indicator you will be evaluated on, you are setting yourself up for failure before you even start. I highly recommend sitting down with your supervisor and asking them how you will be evaluated at the end of the year. If they don't have a clear answer for you, then simply ask: How would you envision my first year being successful? What would they view as a failure? What objectives and expectations do they have for you to meet? What would it look like if you exceeded their expectations? When you ask them these types of questions, be sure to take a pen and paper and write them down. That will become the lens or filter you run everything through as you plan out the days ahead. You may not always get specifics on every area you want from your boss, but at least you will have some direction on how to start heading in the right direction.

There is no step-by-step manual on how to lead, though many have tried. It will be a journey where you will continually evaluate your progress as you move along. What you have done up to this point is what you will lean on and draw from to get started. After the excitement wears off, reality will set in and you will need to step up. It won't always be easy or comfortable, and at times it will feel awkward and clumsy, but that's ok, it's all part of the process of learning to lead. Like a kid who takes off the training wheels for the first time, you may need to ride with both feet off the pedals near the ground to stabilize. Your promotion will provide plenty of opportunities to slow down. Think through what you are doing and receive encouragement when you are heading in the right direction. It may not always be pretty and it may not always be perfect, but don't forget you are now leading. You are in charge!

Making Decisions

You are where you are today in your life because of the decisions you have made up to this point. Whether we like it or not, the decisions we make will make us. Do you want a better life, to lead better, have more influence, make more money? Make better decisions. Where we often get into trouble is not making decisions at all. Not deciding is a decision. I have seen leaders who literally get paralyzed when it comes to decision making. One of my favorite biblical principles on leadership is about making decisions. The principle goes like this: "A double minded man or woman is unstable in all their ways. They will not be blessed."[15] This is a metaphor of someone having two heads. They go back and forth like a bush in the wind when it comes to deciding. One minute they want to go one way, and the very next it's the opposite. Being a double minded leader will not go well for you. It will create instability for you and no one wants to be with you when you are not stable. Following your leadership will be like riding on a rollercoaster. One minute you will be up, the next you will be down. To lead effectively, you will need to improve your decision-making ability. Let's look at five ways we can improve our ability to make better decisions.

1. **Seek Out Guidance and Get Counsel** – one of the quickest and most reliable ways to make better decisions is to ask someone what they would do. If you do this, keep some general guidelines in place beforehand. First, make sure you are asking someone who has a track record of making good decisions. Learning from a seasoned decision-maker will reduce the mistakes you have to make along the way. In a way, you get the "cheat codes" to your problem by asking them for counsel. Second, be selective in the number of people you seek out. Too many voices create confusion and the potential to

make the decision even harder for you. Pick two or three individuals you respect and seek their counsel. Lastly, find at least one person who can be fully objective and brutally honest with you. Don't just seek out those you know who think like you. If someone is too close to the situation and knows too much, it can influence what they say in an effort to please you. They may say what they think you want to hear. Having someone who will not be impacted by your decision directly, and has your best interest at heart, is best.

2. **Start Small** – never overlook the power of small. Many new leaders brush off little responsibilities. Decision making is like building muscle; the more you exercise a muscle the stronger you will become. You talk to any strong man and at one point he was weak. How did he get stronger? Lifting little weights over time that led to bigger weights and more muscle. Years later, the pipsqueak is Mr. Olympia. Look for ways to make smaller decisions. Reorganize a storage closet, volunteer to lead a staff retreat, help with budgeting, be the go-to person for staff communication, or create a project at home. These types of scenarios will create opportunities to make smaller decisions.

3. **Study Leaders From the Past** – be a consumer of different types of literature and study other leaders and how they made decisions. How did they see things when making decisions? What were the main factors they considered before deciding? Did they have a process they followed? How much involvement did they get from their followers? Ultimately, making decisions develops from perspective. The best way to gain a fresh perspective is to learn from someone else. Those who make good decisions see from a different viewpoint, allowing them to act outside the norm and drive positive results.

By studying and learning from leaders in the past, how you view different situations will change for the better. Every decision in your life and leadership will not always be black and white. Wisdom is the ability to operate outside the realm of right versus wrong. You can make the right decision or a wise decision. A right decision may be short lived, but a wise decision has lasting impact. If there is money in your budget to buy new equipment and hire part-time help, it may be a right and good decision to do so. Alternatively, perhaps a wise decision would be not to hire new part-time employees yet but to give raises to those currently on staff. Consult with your staff on how hiring new employees or getting some new equipment would best serve the department. You not only make your department better, but you set it up for success for the long run. When you learn and glean wisdom from those who have gone before you will increase your ability not just to make a good decision but a wise one.

4. **Cut Out the Noise** – today we have way too many outlets that can cause so much noise that many times our minds never have the opportunity to turn off and clear out. A good decision requires a clear mind. Some of the best leaders in our country have rituals and routines of getting alone with their thoughts and quieting their minds. Your mind operates and handles information and interactions and stimulation from the day in your conscious mind. That is the top layer of your thoughts. The subconscious mind operates beneath that. Quieting your mind allows your subconscious mind to operate so you think and see more clearly, and can generate ideas and solutions.

5. **Reflect More Often** – when you get quiet don't just go into a trance and check out. Reflect and think about the decision you need to make. Think through your life and all the relationships and experiences you have had thus far. What problems or mistakes have you made in the past? Have you really learned from them or are you

about to make the same mistake? To make a better decision, reflect on what it will take to follow through. How can you ensure a better outcome? Will this decision require more courage? Will you need to have some difficult conversations with someone? Think through the repercussions and how to manage those? Is there anything you are overlooking currently that you might have missed regarding this decision? Is there someone who needs to be brought up to speed? Again, the purpose here is not to check out mentally, but to really put some thought into your decision and the ramifications.

As you learn to make better decisions, your leadership will improve over time. Not all decisions will be easy, nor will they always yield the intended results. Sometimes, life gets in the way and does its own thing. Even when that happens, stay true to your leadership and keep making good decisions no matter how hard they are. I have learned the harder the decision, the more important it is for me to do what is right.

Managing vs. Leading

As a young boy, I loved riding my bike. It was my vehicle of adventure to take me places I would otherwise never get to visit. Without my bike I would be bored and feel trapped at home with my parents, but inevitably, riding bikes guarantees mechanical problems, and consequently learning to be a bike mechanic on the fly. I enjoyed taking my bike apart and figuring out how it worked. Problems with the back tire were usually related to chain tightness. A chain that wouldn't stay on meant big trouble: no drive and no traction. Stuck like Chuck. Trouble with the front tire was often related to the steering column and increased the danger of running into objects. I became quite comfortable using wrenches and vice grips to adjust and apply pressures in various angles and eventually got really good at fixing my bike and getting it to run like a championship BMX bike. There was no way around it: if I wanted to ride my bike I had to gain the skills to fix it, too.

There is a big difference between managing and leading. Managing is like the back tire of the bike providing traction and power to move you forward. Managing can be monotonous and, at times, boring. The front tire, on the other hand, steers and sets the course of your path. However, each tire is equally important. One without the other and you go nowhere. You need management to get things done, to be disciplined, and to do the daily work. Without management, there is no force to propel you forward. Without a front tire, you would endlessly spin your back tire and go nowhere. There would be no new sights for vision, no new adventures and mountains to climb, and your mission would be over. If you want to lead well, you must understand the difference and importance of each. In learning to manage, you must also learn to lead, motivate and cast a vision for your team and organization. Without leadership you run the risk of losing direction and purpose. Work must get done, but an organization also needs direction to create momentum.

Take a look at the chart below to compare some of the differences between leadership and management.

LEADERSHIP VS. MANAGEMENT[16]	
Leader (front tire)	Manager (back tire)
Copes with change	Copes with complexity
Challenges the status quo	Works with the status quo
Asks why	Asks what
Plans long term	Plans short term
Aligns people	Organizes people
Motivates and inspires	Administrates and controls
Focuses on people	Focuses on systems and structures
Communicates and delivers the vision	Follows the Vision
Looks into the future	Works in the present

When it comes to leadership, keep in mind the importance of knowing the difference between the two. Part of this includes investing in your staff to develop their gifts and strengths. You cannot be the best at everything at all times and you cannot do everything by yourself. Develop a team of people where some are gifted in management and some are gifted in leadership. A diverse group of people working in harmony together keeps people engaged and growing. Having a team without vision can lead to a drop in morale or loss of motivation toward the mission. Alternatively, your vision could be amazing, but if momentum cannot be sustained, frustration sets in. Your team is always starting new initiatives but nothing ever gets finished. You need both management and leadership to be successful over time. <u>Let's look at five principles about leading and managing to help you navigate the differences.</u>

1. **Every Season or Situation May Require You to Be Imbalanced** – just like a bike going up a steep hill will need more work from the back tire, you may go through seasons or situations that require more from a different area. If production is down and there is not a lot of work getting done, you may need to lean more on being managerial. On the other hand, if you are going through some challenging situations or morale drops, you may need more leadership to navigate the terrain. Everything isn't always balanced and distributed evenly all the time. Different seasons and situations often require more from each area.

2. **Lead From Your Strengths and Hire for Your Weaknesses** – get really good at what you do. If you are a great manager and vision is not your thing, be sure to look for some visionaries to bring alongside you. These are usually your creative types, dreamers, and innovators. They tend to ask a lot of questions, push back more times than not, and are always seeing what could be. They tend to make managers uncomfortable because they are always challenging the status

quo. If you are naturally gifted at leadership, realize you will need some good managers to help implement your vision. You can have a world changing vision, but if there is no one organizing a plan of action to make it happen, it is just a dream. It will never get off the ground.

3. **Know How to Both Manage and Lead** – most people are usually geared towards one or the other. There will be times, as a leader and visionary you have to manage. At some point as a manager, you will have to lead and cast vision. You will also be called to communicate, connect with others, and bring inspiration. You don't have to be Tony Robbins, but you will need to learn how to lead at some level. Though you may lean heavily one way or the other, you must learn to do both. As you do this, you will develop a healthy respect for the importance of different skill sets as well as value those who hold different positions and responsibilities than yours.

4. **Find Ways to Create Synergy** – just like the analogy of the two tires that work together to be effective for a bike, so too there must be synergy between leadership and management to be successful. When someone gifted at leading doesn't work well with someone managing it can lead to failure and frustration. If there is a disconnect, it can lead to long term problems down the road. Help your team find common ground to work for and from. Doing this will strengthen the bonds of relationship, respect, and trust. There will be times you need to do this intentionally through team bonding, staff retreats, and strategic planning. Carve out time to ensure your people are connecting and understanding each other on a basic level. When there is good synergy between the two types of people and areas, your staff or team has the potential to become a powerful organization.

5. **Take Inventory** – one way to help distinguish and delineate between leadership and management is to take inventory. You can do this by taking a piece of paper and writing two columns at the top: leadership and management. List everything you do or would like to do underneath one of the two columns. After you have done a brain dump on everything you can think of, then go back through and compare each item on your list. What has been going well for you? What needs more attention or time given to it? What hasn't gone very well for you? Sometimes it can be hard to really see how you are doing unless you sit down and take stock of everything and place it in front of you on paper. By doing this you will gain clarity on what's really going on in all the different areas you oversee.

Just like when I was riding my bike when I was a young boy, sometimes the trips you take are not always exciting. The road is flat, smooth, and straight. The back wheel is doing most of the work. The front wheel is not as involved and it's kind of boring – just keep it straight and on the right path. However, once you go off road and the terrain changes, the front wheel now becomes even more critical and the rush of excitement and focus heightens. It can be just like this for you as well as a leader. Day to day work routines and rituals can be boring and management (back wheel) does all the work. Leadership (front wheel) doesn't seem as necessary and can be unseen. Then all of a sudden, you take on a new initiative, a crisis pops up, or you go through a rough season with a staff member and now leadership (front wheel) is critical. Both wheels are active and needed and emphasis can go back and forth depending on each unique situation and demands. You cannot lead your way into better management and you cannot manage your way into better leadership. Leadership needs good management but management also needs good leadership. The two go hand and hand, depend on each other and must respectfully work together if you are to accomplish your mission and achieve great success.

360 Degree Leadership
(Leading Up – Leading Across – Leading Down)

I remember the first ropes course I went through vividly. We were on a family vacation in Stone Mountain Park, Georgia. I had heard of ropes courses before and how fun they could be, but had never experienced one personally. There were people everywhere, walking, climbing, and suspended from the earth. Of course, my family was chomping at the bit to do it, while I stood back in silence evaluating if I wanted to attempt this or not. My fear of heights caused my stomach to tighten as I weighed my options. I didn't want to even attempt it, to be honest. However, it was our family vacation, and my daughters were intent on making the climb. If I chose to sit out, I would miss the memories and experience with my girls. If my girls were brave enough to do it, there was no way I could say no. I agreed to join in and before I knew it I was in line being fitted for a harness, picking out a helmet, and listening to someone give me safety instructions. My anxiety cranked up several more levels immediately. As I began, I realized something surprising. I was enjoying it. The view was great, my focus locked in, and the adrenaline rush of physically moving through the different challenges of the course was exhilarating. Depending on where you were in the course, you were required to do three things consistently: manage who was to your right and left, keep an eye on the ground below, and, every so often, look up to see what was above you. The laughter, smiles, and gasps we experienced as we completed each section was unforgettable. I am so thankful I faced my fear and joined in.

Leadership and competence are, in many ways, like the ropes course. Once you get the courage to join in, your advancement depends on how well you manage across. Who is climbing with you on your current level? You don't want to knock them off. Who is below you? You don't want to drop something on them. Who is above or ahead of you? Managing who is ahead of you will help you continue to make progress. Not knowing where you are going can cause you to get lost and not make good decisions. You could take a wrong turn very easily. To put it simply, you must be a 360-degree leader. You cannot manage only yourself if you want to move up. You must learn how to manage people at all levels of your organization. <u>Let's look at five simple ways you can learn to be a 360-degree leader to lead up, across and down.</u>

1. **Get Equipped** – the very first thing I got before climbing that day was my equipment. This helped me stay safe and allowed me to navigate the different parts of the course. When I finally got to the highest points of the course, I was grateful for the right equipment. In leadership, we may sign up for something we are ill equipped for and end up in a dangerous or costly career position. The right equipment makes a difference. Luke Skywalker received training from Master Yoda before facing Darth Vader. Though he didn't win the first fight, it saved his life! Take a course on leading, find a mentor, or sign up for a job shadowing opportunity. Get trained and get equipped.

2. **Team Up** – get on a team. When you team up, it forces discussions to center on challenges you are facing. You can problem solve and work through challenges as a group. By working with a team, you will not only get other people's perspectives but you will also work with people who have different strengths and talents.

3. **Get Your Bearings** – similar to my ropes course, you must know where you are at. Without that knowledge, you cannot move forward. Who is beside you? What level are you on, who is above you? Knowing your bearings raises your level of awareness and how your

movement impacts those around you. Not only that, but how others are also reacting helps you make and manage decisions. The adage "crap rolls downhill" is so true. Not knowing who is below you and how your decisions and actions may affect them, can ultimately hurt you.

4. **Communicate to All Levels** – communicate with everyone around you. Whether or not you know them well, your communication, or lack thereof, can set you back. On the ropes course that day, I had to interact and talk to people I had just met. It was uncomfortable, but you know what? I didn't want to get hurt or fall! It's amazing how quickly you can get over your fears when you are feeling pressure in a situation. Most leaders are poor communicators not because they can't do it, but because they don't want to. To lead successfully on all levels, build strong communication skills with those around you.

5. **Have Fun** – leadership can be fun. When you involve others in the process, leading becomes more enjoyable. I could have sat on the bench at the ropes course and watched from afar. I likely would have been miserable, secretly wishing I had done it. Don't forget to have fun. It might be uncomfortable at first, but give it some time. Put in the effort, make some mistakes, and learn from them. As you do, leading becomes more adventurous and fun!

That day on the ropes course I encountered a situation where I was stuck. The person in front of me didn't want to move. Fear had gripped them because of the instability of the next obstacle. It was a tight rope walking section that was fairly high up and you couldn't go around it. Even though he was harnessed to a safety line, it became an impasse for him. With a little coaching, encouragement, and patience from all of us nearby, he eventually conquered his fear. Everyone sighed with relief when he finally made it across. The crazy thing I took away from that experience was we were all stuck in our current positions until he made it across. Nobody was going anywhere until we all slowed down and put our focus and energies into helping him out. People from below encouraged him, those closest to him gave him simple steps to take, and a couple people from above who had just crossed that section provided perspective. That is a great picture of what being a 360 degree leader is. It's getting the focus off of you and onto others helping them in their need. Though you don't always realize it at the moment, even assisting one person at an impasse helps everyone, especially those closest to them. It's a win-win situation. That is why it is so important to learn how to lead like a 360-degree leader. It won't be easy, but I can promise you that the view from the top is much better than sitting on the park bench watching everyone else have fun. Get to climbing.

CHAPTER 6

CAREER STALLERS AND STOPPERS

"If you could kick the person in the pants responsible for most of your trouble, you wouldn't sit for a month."

—

THEODORE ROOSEVELT

Empty Your Cup – Leave Your Ego at the Door

Life has a way of teaching us lessons in places you would never anticipate. When I was finishing school at the University of Georgia and my college football days were over, I wanted to find a hobby that would allow me to stay active. My neighbor told me about a karate class he had been attending and how much he enjoyed it. He invited me to come and check it out sometime. I was hesitant at first, but after hearing his enthusiasm and assurance that I wouldn't get my head kicked off my shoulders, I accepted the invitation. After one lesson, I was hooked. I recall being the least skilled person in the room. I was this huge football player who couldn't punch his way out of a wet paper bag, getting pushed around by some of the smallest people I had ever seen. I realized I had a lot to learn. I continued to attend class and each week my skills improved. I could literally feel the improvement week after week. One thing you have to understand about karate is the belt ranking system for advancement. To advance, you must be tested on a certain number of techniques, forms, and strikes. If you pass the test, you are awarded a new rank or belt that allows you to advance on to more difficult levels. It was just what I needed!

Unfortunately, just as I discovered karate, I got my first job offer and moved across the country to the University of Colorado at Boulder. I was so bummed I couldn't continue taking my karate classes. I had only advanced to yellow belt; I was still a beginner. As fate would have it, I found another karate teacher in Colorado who taught the same style I was learning in Georgia. He lived near Denver, was a third degree black belt, and taught out of his garage twice a week. After one visit to his class I knew this was the place for me. I picked back up where I left off and began advancing through the ranks. After a few years of training and moving up in skill, I was getting closer to testing for my black belt, a very prestigious achievement for karate practitioners. I was unaware, however, that my instructor was concerned about my cockiness. In martial arts, we regularly reference a quote by Bruce Lee: "Empty your cup so that it may be filled."[17] It suggests the attitude of humility required as you advance in rank so you continue to grow and improve. Pride and arrogance stall learning. If a cup is filled up, there isn't room for more. Emptying your cup reminds you to humbly recall there is more to learn. Without realizing it, my pride was about to put me in my place.

I will never forget testing for my black belt. The test lasted four hours, and I was so beat up afterwards I could barely walk the next day. I did terribly. I wasn't prepared for the intensity or exhaustion of the test. Though I passed, I remember feeling so low and down on myself because of how bad I did. My instructor was so gracious and wise with me.

He reminded me the black belt test isn't about you showing how much you know, but how little you know. It is a test of humility. Without humility, you cannot learn and advance. I ate the biggest piece of humble pie that day.

Most of us start out as a yellow belt when it comes to leadership. We are humble. We don't know much at first and we start out as beginners eager to learn. As the years pass and we advance in experience, title, rank, and salary, we are not always aware of the shift in attitude. We can become cocky and arrogant. Pride sneaks in and growth stops. No one wants to work with you because you act as if you know it all. Pride is deceptive and subtle. I love how Pastor Robert Madu says that "Pride is like bad breath, everyone knows you have it but you."[18] Take a look at the chart below and note the subtle differences between pride and humility.

	BIG EGO (PRIDE)	NO EGO (HUMILITY)
1.	Self-serving	Serves others
2.	Uses others	Builds others up
3.	Sees people as expenditures	Sees people as assets
4.	Insecure (overly sensitive to feedback)	Secure (open to feedback)
5.	Loves the spotlight	Shares the spotlight
6.	Takes all or most of the credit	Shares the credit
7.	Cannot admit mistakes	Not afraid to own up to mistakes

The difference between pride and humility can be the difference between failure and success. What you have done up to this point has worked and brought great success. Success has a dangerous side to it, though, which is why it is so important to empty your cup and stay humble. Pride will lie to you as you head down a path of success, but eventually it catches up to you. It always does. Perhaps you know the story of Icarus who, more than anything, wanted to escape the Island of Crete with his father, Daedalus, after they were placed there by the goddess Athena for murder.[19] In a cunning attempt to escape, Daedalus collects bird feathers and fashions two pairs of wings. Daedalus warns his son not to fly too close to the sun because the wax holding the feathers together would melt, and Icarus would fall to his death. If he flew too close to the water, on the other hand, the wings would be weighed down by condensation from the sea, causing them to crash as well. Icarus, in his youthfulness and lack of adherence to his father's warnings, flies too close to the sun, melting the beeswax holding his wings together, plunges into the sea and drowns. Pride will lead to downfall and destruction. Like most things in life, operating in extremes is not good. Icarus was told to fly between the high and the low; living somewhere in the middle requires wisdom. One of my favorite wisdom sayings is by King Solomon, "When pride comes, then comes disgrace, but with humility comes wisdom."[20] As a leader, it takes a great deal of wisdom to navigate through challenging situations and scenarios. <u>Let's take a look at the top five ways to empty your cup and stay humble.</u>

1. **Walk With a Limp** – never trust a leader who doesn't walk with a limp. The day after my black belt test I was limping and could barely walk. I wasn't as good as I thought I was. That test humbled me and brought me back down to earth. It was a lesson I desperately needed to learn. In the same way, we should be cautious about following any leader who has all the answers and claims to never have made a mistake. If they "have it all figured out" and they are a self-titled "guru," take note. The longer I live and the more I walk with great leaders, this is one trait I look for. Practically speaking, walking with

a limp means you have made some mistakes and learned some lessons from your mistakes. You have been through some struggles and difficulties. You have had some failures that you aren't afraid to admit and own up to. Anytime someone tells me they haven't had any failures or made some mistakes or struggled at all, run! Your cup gets emptied real quick when your ego gets a little too big and something in life reels you in. As my Dad used to say to me growing up in Tennessee, "You get the slack jerked out of your chain!" As you move up and gain success as a leader, you will also need a healthy dose of some setbacks, failures, and mistakes. It will help keep you humble. If you don't experience this early on in your career you will pay a price for it later down the road. I have witnessed people who have had unbridled success for a long time and eventually self-destruct because they didn't experience enough humbling situations as they rose to prominence. They, like Icarus, climbed too fast. That is why it is vital to make sure you don't promote someone too soon. If not done progressively and with caution, it can do more harm than good.

2. **Take the Test and Learn the Lesson** – there will be seasons of your life as a leader when you will be tested. Sometimes you are aware of it and can see it coming but most of the time it happens without notice. In a similar way, when you are tested and you refuse to heed the lesson, you will continue to take the same test over and over again. The day I was tested by my instructor, I had no idea of what I was in for and wasn't fully prepared. Afterwards, I very clearly saw my weaknesses: my cockiness, arrogance, and overinflated view of my skills held me back. Without the test, I may have never seen it myself. Great leaders are tested. How you handle promotion, praise, influence, and power will be a litmus test of your pride. How you treat others, especially those who cannot do anything for you will

say a lot about you as a leader. How you manage failures, flops, and fumbles is a test of maturity. Do you only like receiving acclaim from others and get defensive with criticism and feedback? Pay attention to these little tests in your leadership as you continue to grow and develop. Often, the work done in you is way more important than the work done through you.

3. **Swallow Your Pride** – doing so is difficult, and for some it might feel impossible but I cannot tell you how much trouble, grief, or embarrassment could be avoided if someone would just swallow their pride, admit their mistake, and apologize. When we fail to admit mistakes, we are hurting ourselves the most. We pay the price, not the other person. I understand being fearful of appearing weak or incompetent, but you face a bigger problem if you cannot swallow your pride. Nobody wants to help you if you point the finger at someone else. If you really want to lead, it will take a lot of people to help you get there. You cannot make it happen on your own. At different stages and junctions of your career, you will need a helping hand to take the next step and not swallowing your pride can stop your career dead in its tracks.

4. **Guard Against False Humility** – this one is sneaky but easily detected. If you are someone who cannot accept credit and always give it away, that's false humility. C. S. Lewis defines real, authentic humility the best when he said "True humility is not thinking less of yourself, it's thinking of yourself less."[21] If you have a problem with receiving compliments and credit and are always dismissing it to someone else, watch out. False humility isn't believable and it sends a message to others you are trying too hard to come across

as humble. Take credit for what you've done and thank those who helped you. There is nothing wrong with doing so and it blesses the person giving you credit as well. Not receiving credit for a job well done is really pride trying to hide itself.

5. **Choose The Right People** – prideful leaders surround themselves with "yes" people. They need those who will agree with and go along with them. In these environments, there is only one way of doing things, they have to make all the decisions, and they are the only ones with good ideas, which means they also hoard the credit. That day I tested out for my black belt, my instructor surrounded me with opponents he knew were better than me. At the time, my pride convinced me they weren't better than me. My instructor knew they were exactly the people I needed to teach me humility. In the same way, surround yourself with others better than you. These are people not afraid to tell you the truth and be honest with you. They will look out for you and have your best interest at heart, not always telling you what you want to hear. The truth isn't always pleasant to hear, but it keeps your ego in check. We all have blind spots. We can put a man on the moon but we still cannot see the back of our necks. Surround yourself with people who aren't afraid to be honest with you.

In summary, emptying your cup is all about keeping a level of humility in your leadership. Over the years, humility has gotten a bad wrap as making someone weak and easy to take advantage of, but in reality, humility doesn't weaken your leadership, it strengthens it. It makes you better. The stronger you are as a leader, the softer you can afford to be. That night I received my black belt, I didn't just move up. I stepped down. I softened in my approach. I finally realized how little I knew and how much more I had to learn. I wasn't lacking skills to advance, I was lacking humility. Pride had blocked me from advancing and like any great teacher, my instructor made sure I would learn the lesson. Empty your cup. Guard your leadership against pride. Stay humble and hungry. Leave your ego at the door.

Destination Disease

Every summer growing up, we would take a family vacation. This usually involved my dad driving our large family in the Dodge minivan with the ginormous, Beverly hillbillies luggage carrier on top, overstuffed with suitcases down the highway with the Rand McNally fold out road map in hand. There was no GPS back then, and for the most part you never really knew how far you had traveled or how close you were to your destination. We had a blended family with seven people, and every single one of us hated sitting in a packed car. For hours or end, there was no room to stretch and even less direction from Dad, our fearless leader. Every road trip would end in a repetitive tirade of the same question: "Are we there yet??" The younger the kid, the more often they asked the question as if that was going to speed up the trip. As the oldest, I had a better sense of time and direction and kept my mouth shut. Looking back on those trips, the restless boredom makes sense. Back then, we didn't have cell phones, DVD players, or video games to help pass the time. You stared out the window for hours, pestered your siblings, played "I spy" or some other made-up game to keep your mind preoccupied during the tortuous road trip. In a recent study, people were tested with two options to choose from.[22] They could sit there alone in their thoughts for fifteen minutes bored, or push a button to shock themselves during the allotted time. Amazingly, a large majority of people chose to be shocked while waiting. People hate to wait and be bored. They would rather feel pain that distracts from the waiting and boredom more than experience the boredom.

This story illustrates a point for all of us. We must be careful with getting "destination disease". Destination disease is always looking for the next place to go without enjoying the journey. I have seen countless leaders get a brand-new job, title, or assignment, and months later, or even weeks, are already restlessly looking for their next gig. They never can settle in and enjoy where they are. They are constantly looking for something better and brighter out there. This is not to say you cannot look for a better job or keep an eye out for an opportunity, but there is a difference in looking with an eye of curiosity versus an eye of discontentment. One keeps you motivated and the other will steal your joy. One thing to keep in mind when it comes to getting promoted is that oftentimes, the process takes longer than you prefer and comes at a time you least expect it. Additionally, your career growth can happen in layers and phases much like the road trip our family would take on vacation each summer. There will be parts of it that are boring, monotonous, and painful. Working through those periods will be key for you as you continue to move up in your career. The grass may seem greener on the other side but it's because someone has been watering it consistently. If your grass isn't green maybe, you should try watering it more often. You would be amazed at how much better the current role and job you are in now would be so much better if you stopped looking in the future for the next big job and make the job you are in the big job. Let's look at five ways to avoid getting "destination disease" as leaders:

1. **Commit to a Longer Period of Time to Stay** – when you get destination disease without even realizing it, you are unconsciously unplugging and pulling back from your current role and job. You may be doing the work, but your heart isn't in it. When this begins to happen, slowly but surely you will begin to be unhappy and it will negatively impact the quality of the work you do, the depth of your relationships, and perspective towards decisions you make daily. One of the biggest things you can do as a leader is set a considerable time commitment to stay in your current job before looking

elsewhere again. To be fair, two or three years is realistic and recommended. Usually, any job you take that is new has about a year or more acclimation period where you actually get settled in and learn the culture, people, and processes. Long term impact takes time and commitment from you and will not happen overnight. Setting a longer time period will force you to let your roots go down deep in the role you are in and bloom where you are planted.

2. **Layout Some Projects and Goals You Want to Accomplish** – just like our trip as kids, we enjoyed the journey so much more when we had a purpose or something to keep us occupied. To ward off destination disease, laying out some key objectives, goals, or projects you want to accomplish will help you firm up your commitment to staying put for a season. When you do this, don't just make the goals self-serving either. Develop yourself, learn and grow but also do something that will last beyond your leadership when you do end up leaving. I remember when we bought our first house in Texas years ago. I intended to leave the house in a better condition than I found it. Eleven years later after a new kitchen, refurbished bathrooms, renovated siding and paint, as well as back porch, the day we moved out it was way better than when we moved in. Take that same approach in your current role. Make the job better, and bigger than when you first arrived. Not only will you be better for it, but the impact you can have will be long lasting and help others.

3. **Build Community in the City You Are In** – the other thing to consider that can happen when you get destination disease is you stop actively pursuing relationships within the community. By community, I mean people outside your normal circles at work. Work relationships are great but they are convenient and don't require much effort on your part. Building a community takes investment of your time and money. Once you start, it demonstrates how invested you

are in making a difference and not just looking to pass through. Actively look for different communities to get involved in outside work. This could be a local church, a non-profit organization, a workout or fitness group, a book club, a humane shelter, or local school to serve in. No matter what you choose, commit to helping and being a part of that community consistently and watch how many friends you make. Your level of happiness and contentment will rise. When we bring balance into our lives, our work life will often improve as a result.

4. **Buy a House** – I have seen leaders move into town with their new job, paycheck and staff, but continue to rent an apartment. They never really put down roots and remain restless. There is something about buying a house that says, "I'm here to stay for a while". I was recently talking to a coach who bought a brand new house and moved out of a rental home. "We wanted to buy a home because we want to be here for a while," he told me. Recently, he was in the market for a new job and while he was almost hired elsewhere, he instead received a nice promotion at his current job, and decided it was time to settle down for a season. I have seen a change in him, not only in his demeanor but in his language, relationships, and how much heart he now puts into his job. Buying a home can help focus your energy, attention, and commitment in a way nothing else can. When you buy a home, you begin to dream, plan, invest, and envision the next season of your life in the neighborhood and community you live in.

5. **Change Your Outlook From "Out There" to "Right Here"** – make a decision to stop looking for happiness out there somewhere. When you are always looking for something else that is out *'there'*, you are saying *'here'* isn't good enough. Perhaps you catch yourself

saying variations of the following:"When I get that job, I will finally have arrived,"

"If I could work at such and such a place, I will be much better off than here."

"If I could work with so and so, I will be way better off than with these people." You spend most of your time looking for a place called "someday" which never arrives. Make your day today. Stop looking for tomorrow and live in the now. Be planted where your feet are. Enjoy the journey. Success in life is never a place we reach and live at. Success is all about the journey! When we forget that, we are discontent and unhappy. Life is too short, time is too precious, and the people we can influence and impact around us need us more than we realize.

It is ok to look for a new job, opportunity, and career path. There is nothing wrong with that, and there is a right time to do so. However, be careful you don't fall into the trap of always looking for the next best thing. As a leader of people and manager, I usually get concerned if I see a track record of short stints and stops at a bunch of different jobs. It raises a flag and I wonder how long they will stay here if we hire them. Most leaders are looking for good people who stay. Employers need a longer term of commitment. Some jobs, like contract laborers, don't fall into this category. To make a lasting impact requires a commitment to settle in and stop looking on the other side of the fence. If we are not careful, promotion can become like it was for us as kids on vacation. We only are doing it for the destination, always looking out for what we want and what makes us happy.

Getting Punked –
When You Don't Get the Promotion You Wanted

When someone got the best of you we would laugh and say, "You got punked!" As kids, getting punked didn't always mean a physical fight broke out, but occasionally it did if it was an intense confrontation. Either way, you never wanted to get punked growing up. The embarrassment, loss of respect, and cool points you could lose from your peers might be unrepairable. No matter what you did as a kid, you avoided getting punked at all costs.

At some point you will face the letdown of not getting a job you applied for. Dealing with the dynamics and difficulties of not getting promoted can be so challenging and severe that you seriously might consider changing professions or getting out altogether. It can take you to the brink of quitting. Missing out on a promotion usually hurts even more if you are qualified and really want the job. Unfortunately, most of us will experience this at some point. As a young, ambitious coach I applied for an opening for a higher-level position working with our baseball team. It was a better salary, a successful team, and a role with more autonomy and visibility. My boss encouraged me to apply for it, even though the head baseball coach was making the decision, and not my boss himself. The head baseball coach would make the decision. I applied and interviewed for the position. I had a great feeling about it. I knew all the people involved in the process, had a great reputation as a strength coach and was trusted within the department. I thought I had a great shot at getting it. I was one of the finalists for the job and got to interview with the head coach. I even felt like we connected and hit it off that day. However, the one thing I lacked was experience with the team I would be training. I had not worked much with baseball players. I ended up not getting the job. I got punked and everyone knew it, too. I was so discouraged and defeated. I replayed over and over what I must have done wrong in the interview. Was it something I said? Was it something I did or didn't do? I felt so rejected and discouraged. I remember thinking if I can't win a job within my department where I am loved, how will I be able to ever get promoted. It will never happen.

To help you avoid stopping or stalling out your career when disappointment hits, let's look at five healthy responses you can have when you don't get the promotion.

1. **It's Not the End of the World** – keeping a good perspective will help you get through the disappointment. Don't think *why* I did not get the job, think *when* will I get the job! No doesn't mean never, it just means not now. If you keep your head on straight, the disappointment could prepare you for a future promotion. But you say, "I wanted this one! It was my dream job!" Here's a secret: your dream job is never the job you think it will be. It may appear dreamy and wonderful, but once you sit in the seat and start putting out fires, your attitude changes quickly. The fact remains: not getting something you want is not the end of the world. You will wake up tomorrow, you will still have a job, and your time will eventually come.

2. **Stay Positive** – a positive attitude can help you navigate disappointment. It's easy to get negative when your feelings are hurt, and you want to crawl in a hole and hide. Don't do it. It will only make it worse. It's ok to feel the pain of disappointment but don't let it cloud your outlook. Stay up and keep your focus. Being negative will suck the life out of you and bring you down. It will prolong the process of you getting a shot at something else to come your way. It's ok to vent and get it out, but after that, get back on track. Nursing disappointment can lead to bitterness and resentment, which spills over into other areas of your life. Staying positive in a negative situation is a must if you want to get promoted. When a plane goes through a storm it flies by an instrument called the "attitude". The attitude tells the captain if the nose of the plane is up or down in a storm with little to no visibility. Keeping the nose up on a plane will ensure the plane is climbing above the clouds so the captain can see again. Keep your head up and stay positive. You will eventually rise above.

3. **Pause and Reflect** – during moments of defeat, don't just wallow in self-pity. Use this time to pause and reflect. What are some valuable lessons you can learn from this experience? How can it make you better? What needs to change moving forward? Can you get some feedback from those involved in the process to help you better prepare for the next time? Think about the job you currently have. What are some of the things you have taken for granted? Are there any ways you can restructure your current position to keep you excited until the promotion does come? Are there any areas you can discuss with your boss that you want to work on? There is always good in not getting the job. It all depends on how you see your situation. When I didn't get the baseball job, it forced me to really dig in and work on my current position. I still had some growing and learning to do. If you stay humble and pause and reflect, this can be a season of growth for you like no other. Don't waste it because you are in a hurry and didn't take time out to pause, reflect, and learn.

4. **It Wasn't Meant to Be** – I know this may sound cliche and too simplistic, but it's true. If you don't get the job for whatever the reason, it just wasn't in the cards for you. It wasn't meant to be. If they don't want you there for that position, trust me you don't want to be there either. Once an employer goes in a different direction and they don't choose you, as hard as it sounds, it's just not meant to be. It's not your time, and it's not the job you need or want. This response will help you put a bow on it and move forward. The hardest thing you can do sometimes is pick up the pieces and move on. As hard as it may be, you must do it. Don't delay. Don't hang out or camp out. Get going again. Seeing the loss of getting the job you wanted in this light will help you move forward.

5. **Deepen Your Commitment** – when you don't get promoted, it will do one of two things: make you give up or motivate you to rise

higher. Some of the most discouraging and disappointing times in my career when seeking new positions have led to some of the most focused, productive, and fulfilling seasons of my job. Nothing will motivate you more than falling short of reaching a desired goal. Doing everything in your power to pursue the job and promotion you wanted only to come up short will light a fire under you like no other. Some questions to ask yourself: How bad do I really want it? What are some little extra things I can do to move me closer? Where has my commitment grown weak? Where have I become complacent? Where can I step up my game? What areas can I sharpen my skill sets? Who can I network with for mentoring? Adopting this mindset is the only way I have seen that works. I have tried it the other way and it never works. Not doing anything gets you exactly that, nothing. It only leaves you more despondent and hopeless for a better future. By deepening your commitment, not only will you feel better but you will stay in the driver's seat of your career, and build the momentum you need for when your time does come. Momentum will be attractive to those in hiring positions. They will not only see your skills and talents you possess, but they will also pick up on you as the type of individual who will come in and continue to improve and get better.

Getting punked will happen. You will not be able to avoid it. Just don't let it stop you. Right now doesn't mean no or never. Get knocked down seven times, rise eight times. It will take courage and conviction on your part to take the hits and keep coming. Coach Tony Dungy said it best when he said, "Courage is the ability to do the right thing all the time, no matter how painful or uncomfortable it might be."[23] As you begin reaching for the goal of getting promoted, take courage my friend. Don't quit, don't give in. Your time will eventually come.

CHAPTER 7

PERSONAL DEVELOPMENT

"One quality of leaders and high achievers in every area seems to be a commitment to ongoing personal and professional development."

—

BRIAN TRACY

Work Harder on Yourself Than You Do On Your Job

I was nineteen the first time I came home from college at the University of Georgia. I had spent a little over a year going to school, training hard to put on size, strength, and speed to earn a spot for some playing time. All that year, I worked and worked and worked and never really felt like I was getting much bigger. I knew I was getting stronger and had added some weight but every time I looked in the mirror I was discouraged. When I went home and ran into some of my old teammates from high school, their jaws dropped when they saw me. "D. Maib holy $hit what have you been doing? You have gotten HUGE!?" I looked at them with excitement and said "Really"? They were like "Dude, we almost didn't recognize you. You have put on some mass!"

When you work on yourself and make it a priority to grow and get better every single day, you don't notice your own improvement. You want to feel like you are making progress, but it's incremental and small. Plus, since it's so slow and you see yourself every day, you don't notice it. Over time though, others will take notice! Jim Rohn once said, "Work harder on yourself than you do on your job". That season at Georgia all I did was work on myself. I knew I was smaller, weaker, and slower and that created a sense of urgency for me. I worked harder on myself than anything else and eventually it paid off. It took longer than I expected, was harder than I could have imagined, but it was worth it.

When we start off on our leadership journey, many of us feel like I did during that season at Georgia. We are new employees, behind in our skills and knowledge, and low on the totem pole. We read, study, take courses, get mentored and go the extra mile to sharpen ourselves and get ready for our next step. As we make progress towards our advancements, we start to focus more on doing our jobs while our responsibilities and personal goals tend to take a back seat. What gave us an edge early on, can be lost quickly if we stop working on ourselves. The same way you move up, you can slide back down if you are not careful. Keeping the hunger and drive to improve and grow will be critically important as you look to move up. As you get more experienced and know more, you will need to be creative to stay sharp. You will need to be intentional and stay curious. Getting bigger titles, offices, staff to manage, and increased access to resources can make you lazy and complacent. I have seen this happen to leaders and have personally experienced what can happen if you let up. If you want to move up and keep advancing in your career, there is no other way around it. Work harder on yourself than you do on your job. <u>Let's look at five reasons why this is a must if you want continued growth as a leader:</u>

1. It Kills Complacency – too many people today get satisfied and relax when they get to a place where they don't have to push as much. I am not saying you can't ever relax and take a breath and enjoy the position you have. You should enjoy it especially if you sacrificed to get there. However, things in life tend to either get better or worse with time. If you don't believe me, go on a month-long vacation, and see how your yard looks when you get back and nobody cares for it. If you are not careful, complacency creeps in. You will get way too comfortable and think because you have reached a certain position, that you can just coast and not work as hard anymore. The greatest threat to tomorrow's success is today's success. Complacency is the silent career killer. Once that begins to happen you will start to lose your edge. Don't settle. Stay hungry. Keep working, learning, and growing.

2. **It Will Keep Your Passion Alive** – I love my job. One of the reasons is because I never stop learning. I am constantly reading books, listening to podcasts, meeting with other coaches, and traveling to new cities. Sometimes, I feel like a big kid. The more I do this, the more I realize how much I don't know and how much there is still to learn and improve. It fires me up, stokes my hunger, and motivates me to be the best I can be. On the other hand, I have had seasons where I was flat, dry, and bored. I wasn't very motivated and on the edge of burn out. I would think, "Why am I struggling, why am I not excited anymore, where has my passion gone?" For me, it always came back to one thing; I had stopped working on myself and was on autopilot. I was losing my edge and I could feel it. You can and will too if you don't watch it. It is a very subtle thing and sneaks up on even the best of leaders.

3. **It's Infectious** – a spark from a fire can start another fire. Some of the largest forest fires were begun by some bystander flipping a small cigarette into a dry grass field. You would be astounded how

infectious it is to be around someone who works to better themselves consistently. People will love being around you. When you are constantly growing and learning, what you put in naturally comes out. I often see leaders giving back to others but never putting anything back into themselves. The more you put in, the more you can give out of yourself. The more life you give, the more others want to be and enjoy being around you. Some of the most influential leaders and mentors I have had the privilege to learn from emulated this quality. I could spend hours around them and it felt like only a few minutes. Continually pour into yourself. Place the oxygen mask on yourself first, then others second.

4. **The Best Always Get Better** – no matter what area of life you investigate and research, the best are always getting better. Athletics, business, ministry, music, medicine, technology and on and on. Those at the top of their game and industry continue to find creative and innovative ways to improve and level up their game. The problem is that people think they want to be the best, but all they do is talk about it. They don't do the work required to be the best. When you are fully committed to being and doing the best you can, it is hard work. It's not always fun and games, but the fruit of your efforts is so fulfilling in the long run.

5. **It Will Take You Places You've Never Dreamed Of** – when you work on yourself consistently you can expect adventure. I cannot count the times I have met a new leader or influencer, traveled to a new city, or gained a new insight on an old topic that surprised me. Part of your growth and learning process is staying curious and maintaining a sense of adventure. Any pioneer who blazes a new trail, doing something that's never been done, has a heart for adventure. They wanted to go places no one has ever been, and they wanted to accomplish the things someone said couldn't be done. There

was something in them that hated the status quo. Maybe you won't scale large mountains or leap through flames to keep your edge, but be vigilant with your growth and development so that you don't risk growing stagnant, stale, and irrelevant. Stay curious.

Take a moment and reflect on where you are currently. What was the last book you read that fired you up and got you excited? How is your drive and motivation these days? Who are you currently learning from in business and in life? What stretch goals have you set that inspire you and push you out of your comfort zone? Are you looking forward to the next phase of your career or are you wanting to retire? Even if you are older and closer to retirement, you still don't want to simply fade off into the sunset. Retire inspired! Don't retire from something, retire to something. No matter what age, season of life, and situation you are currently in, guard and keep your passion alive to keep growing, improving, and bettering yourself. It is the key to life, to success, and most importantly your happiness. That is the difference between a career and a calling. It's not just something you get paid for, it is something you were made for!

Creative Ways to Develop Yourself

In the early 1970s and 1980s there was an exercise consultants were using called the "9 Dot Puzzle" (see below).[24] It was three rows of three dots each, and the goal was to try and draw four straight lines to connect all the dots without lifting the pencil or tracing backwards over a line already drawn.

This exercise coined the cliché term "Think Outside the Box". The purpose of the exercise was to try and teach others how to think differently, unconventionally, or with a new perspective. One of the solutions to solving the problem clearly shows that once you get outside the shape of the "box" the solution is clear.

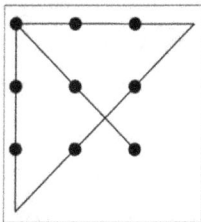

By drawing outside the uniform shape of the

dots, the challenge is easily solved. To think outside the box is to look further and try new things. A crucial part of your leadership journey will be developing yourself. If you make the time to devote yourself to personal growth, the chances of your success and growth as a leader will increase significantly. To do this you will need to think outside the box. The days of linear thinking are over. Applying for an internship, getting your masters, studying and gaining accreditation, and applying for jobs are examples of linear thinking and while these are standard benchmarks for qualifications to get a position, you will need to look into other, more creative avenues to develop professionally.

Early on in your career, you need to take time and learn a lot about a little. You will need to pick one area and get really good at it. After some time, if you want to get promoted, you need to change your focus and learn a little about a lot. In other words, you will need to broaden your range of knowledge and expertise. This will require you to move from being a specialist (having depth in one area of expertise) to a generalist (creating width in many areas of expertise). In the book "Range" by David Epstein, he shows in his current research the value of increasing our "range" whether we are problem solving or training athletes; the best answers and solutions are not always found in our specialty but outside of it.[25] If we only look for solutions in our current industry, we limit our options for innovation, growth and solutions to problems we face. I have seen this happen in my profession over the years as a coach. In order for someone to move up into a higher role, greater knowledge and experience would need to be gained. If they didn't, they would remain stuck in the same position and eventually burn out. Areas like project management, budgeting, casting vision, dealing with contractors, and marketing would have helped them move up in their career. They wouldn't have needed to know a ton about all these areas, but they would need to know a little about each. Simply put, develop yourself by looking and learning from other areas or industries other than the one you are currently in. Think outside the box when it comes to your career. Creatively developing yourself will pay huge dividends for you as a leader. <u>Let's look at five benefits of why you need to be creative in developing yourself.</u>

1. **Thinking Differently** – you will never move or live beyond your thought life. Every great invention, gadget, product, and idea started out as a thought. If you don't change how you think you will get one thing in return: stuck! Too many people today are stuck in their careers because they refuse to think differently. Not only do you need to think differently, you need to think BIG! Small thinking is stinking thinking. I recall the story I read years ago in the book by Lou Tice called "Personal Coaching for Results".[26] In the book, Tice tells a story about a farmer who won the pumpkin growing contest at the county fair one year. His pumpkin was shaped like a jug. When the judge asked him how he got the pumpkin in the shape of the jug, he responded "I grew the pumpkin seed inside a jug." It's the same in our brain as well. Your career will follow your thoughts. It is mission critical to think differently.

2. **You Need New Environments for Stimulation and Inspiration** – you cannot give what you do not have. If all you do is the same thing every day of the week, every month of the year you will never grow at the rate you need to. Putting yourself in different environments is healthy for you. It will challenge you, get you out of your comfort zone regularly, and protect you from getting stagnant in your career. If our job is to challenge others and help them improve, we must practice what we preach. New environments foster growth and improvement and can be an impetus towards greater learning. Staying in the "same old, same old" type of environment can cause atrophy and lethargy. Consistent work habits and routines are vital for stability and incremental progress, but if you want to continually

grow and develop as a leader, seek out new environments to inspire, educate, and propel you forward.

3. **You Need to Meet New People** – leadership is relational and dynamic in nature. If you are not regularly seeking out new people to meet or learn from, you are cutting off oxygen to your soul. The challenges of meeting new people are time, space and money. Our schedules are packed, we fail to create the space to do it consistently, or we lack the resources to make it happen. With technology, however, everyone is within reach. They are a text or direct message away. You can Zoom or FaceTime just about anybody at any time. The creative piece comes down to your hustle. It may require you to work a little extra to get someone's attention or contact. You may have to work through several contacts to set up a meeting with an expert in your field. It never ceases to amaze me after all these years how closely connected we all are. What if the very person you know, knows someone you need to meet and help unlock your career. It will require you to do some homework, and meet with some of your associates to see who they might know who could help you. Being creative in developing yourself requires intentional conversations with others about your goals and objectives in life. To go a step further, there are so many great leaders, thinkers, and historians you can learn from and mentors that are no longer alive. Learning from those who have led through situations you are currently going through can have a profound impact on your growth and development. I have gleaned a lot over the years studying Martin Luther King Jr., Abraham Lincoln, and Marcus Aurelius. Though no longer alive, they still speak to me today.

4. **You Need to Fail More Often** – though not popular today, we learn far more from our failures than our successes. If we stop failing, we stop learning. If we stop learning, we stop growing. Coaches and

leaders more concerned about how they are perceived or who gets the credit will avoid failure at all costs. The struggles and difficulties you go through will strengthen you the most. Muscles do not get stronger without resistance and struggle. The very simple concept of adaptation illustrates how your body, when weakened and broken down by resistance, engages the brain to put processes in place to rebuild it stronger. In the coaching industry, we "periodize", or plan out, cycles of pushing people beyond their comfort zone so they can improve. In the same way you have periodization for athletes training cycles with heavier weeks than others, so your career needs times and seasons where it's harder and more difficult. It is much better to strive for big goals and come up short than to set small goals and not do anything. Pushing yourself and failing from your attempts will create great opportunities for growth. The key is to create enough tension so that you struggle, but not so much tension that you get crushed. A goal just outside your reach is best. Everyone has different tensions and levels of adversity they can handle; being aware of your limitations is a big part of developing yourself creatively. You will learn more about your weaknesses as you push yourself beyond what you think you can handle. One of the best development positions I took on was leading and directing our football summer camps. My boss didn't think I could handle it with all the other responsibilities on my plate, and honestly, I wasn't so sure at the time either. However, I knew putting myself in a new, challenging situation would force me into positions and places I had never been. That summer I failed more than I had before, but what it gave me was confidence and insight I could not have gotten any other way. I had to deal with hiring and managing staff, balancing a budget, creating new policies, disciplining and leading kids who were unmotivated, receiving criticism from unhappy parents, and many other unpleasant experiences. What others viewed as a negative opportunity became a catalyst for my growth and stepping stone to becoming a better leader.

5. **You Need to Be More Entrepreneurial** – Working outside your normal day job is very beneficial. At your current job, everything is there for you already. You report to a boss, or supervisor, who helps to keep you on track. And, resources are already there for you, even if it's not much. Others you work with already know you and see you in a certain light and you can get the flow down pretty quick. On the other hand, being entrepreneurial will help develop your hustle. You will have to be a self-starter. You will have to develop more discipline and think creatively. Resources will be more scarce and not always within reach. You will encounter obstacles and barriers. The level of persistence and resilience required to be successful will be greater than you imagined. I am not saying you have to be an entrepreneur, but I am saying you need to have some side gigs going on. For years I have struggled with this concept, but finally, I have come to the reality that having a hobby or passion you pursue to generate income will provide a wealth of capital in career development as you go. I am writing this book as a result of all the years of my speaking and doing presentations. Something I have truly enjoyed for so many years continues to push me and help me grow in areas I wouldn't have dreamed of. Often we refuse to pursue something because we are not good at it or we just don't want to invest the time into it because it will take so long to improve. For most of us, starting anything new will be difficult at first. It's awkward, we don't know exactly what to do, and others may not approve when we take that first step. If we can push past the discomfort and maintain the energy and drive to find something that is entrepreneurial, it will pay huge dividends in growth and development. What hobbies can you dabble in and make some extra money at? Maybe it's

photography, or cooking. Do you enjoy hiking and nature? Are there some community groups you can get involved in and provide services for? Do you really enjoy traveling or working with animals? It could even be something like collecting baseball cards or studying sport stats. I always like to say, find something you enjoy doing so much that you would do it for free and then get so good at it that someone will pay you money to do it! Find something even if it's small and insignificant. If you are only five percent entrepreneurial you will benefit from that way more than not trying at all. The biggest growth that goes unnoticed is incremental.

Think outside the box. Today's job market and career path isn't as linear as it was twenty years ago. Our paths are more fluid and career options have increased drastically, with more ways to make a living. Becoming a better person should be the end goal. Yes, you need more skills, more knowledge, more insight, and more relationships but ultimately you need to become bigger as a human being. You need to be more patient, kind, thoughtful, loving, passionate, assertive, and optimistic. To become who you want to become, there is only one way: do things you have never done! Think outside the box.

Horrible Bosses

One of my first bosses was horrible. Well, at least that's what I thought as a young teenager working my first summer job in a plastics factory one summer in Tennessee. At the time I was nineteen years old and had just completed my freshman year at Georgia. College was not what I thought it would be. It was far harder and not as fun as I had anticipated. I was entertaining the thought of not going back to school. I could just become a normal person, get a job, and move on with life. Problem solved. Until I met my first factory supervisor "Broom Hilda" that summer. To this day I cannot recall her name, but I will forever be grateful for that factory and what she did for me. "Broom Hilda" was mean, aggressive, and very unapproachable. To give her some credit, she was very young herself and was overseeing a bunch of older men who quite frankly didn't work hard, showed up late, and were half intoxicated when they did show up. She had a tough job. After working under her for one summer, my attitude and perspective about school changed completely. It was the best thing that could have ever happened to me. Life can be funny like that sometimes. We think we got it so bad in our current situation or job, until you experience something much worse. Then, all of a sudden, what you have isn't so bad after all. That was exactly what happened to me. I got a checkup from the neck up! If you have any aspirations or goals to lead in any capacity you will have to live through or deal with a bad boss.

Before we go too much further, let's define what I mean by a horrible boss. As I have matured through the years, my understanding and perspective has changed drastically about my former bosses. When I was young and lacked experience, I didn't fully understand why my bosses made the decisions they did, and I misjudged them. We can be overly critical and lack perspective because we are not fully involved in conversations, know all the details, or having to deal with our boss's boss. There are so many factors that can influence a leader's demeanor and decision making process at any given moment. Just because one or two people don't like their boss's style of leading or managing doesn't make them a horrible boss. There are no perfect bosses. All bosses are human and they have weaknesses or blind spots. I'm not talking about styles or weaknesses here.

A horrible boss is someone who is negligent. They don't look out for their people. They use others to serve themselves and take advantage. Those underneath their leadership do not flourish. They do not feel appreciated or celebrated for their dedication and effort. Whether they are aware of it or not, they treat people disrespectfully, erode trust and do very little if anything to show employees they are valued and appreciated. When you have a horrible boss, the entire unit or department will feel it. It won't just be two or three people feeling sorry for themselves. Morale will be low, complacency and mediocrity will settle in, and no one will look forward to coming to work.

Working for a horrible boss can be bad, but what can be worse is to work under a leader like that and waste your time. As I mentioned, at some point you will have to deal with a bad boss. That's just how life works. The worst thing you could do is go through a season of your career under poor leadership and not grow from it and learn from it. I have learned so many valuable lessons and gained more personal growth in all my years of coaching not just from great leaders, but also from bad bosses. <u>Let's look at five positives for working under a horrible boss that can help you grow your leadership.</u>

1. **Teach You What Not to Do** – when you work under a bad boss, you get to experience first-hand what it feels like to be hurt, mistreated, left out and let down. Though it can have a negative impact on you at the time, if you let it, you will develop a compassion inside of you that people will be drawn to. When you personally know the pain of what it feels like to be hurt, you will take great care in how you treat others as you move up. As humans, we typically learn compassion and have the best understanding towards those we have suffered like us in similar ways. If you have ever been yelled at, disrespected, overlooked, marginalized, taken advantage of or demoted, you know what it feels like to hurt. If you can forgive, learn from it, stand up for yourself, and grow from it you will be a much better leader because of it. You will be better prepared to lead others.

2. **Manage Up** – one of the best skills you must learn as a leader is how to manage up. I honestly did not learn this until later in my career and no one ever told me about it. I had to learn it the hard way. Most bad bosses are not aware they are a bad boss, and if you don't

manage them and their weaknesses, you will pay for it. If they are unapproachable, find a way to connect with them. Avoiding them and running from them will only make things worse for you and you will get replaced. Find a way to get closer to them. You might be thinking, "You are crazy! I don't want to be closer to them." For years I took this approach and I suffered because of it. Find a way to connect with them. Volunteer for a project where you have to check in with them regularly. Schedule a meeting with them to ask a question or give an update. Watch and study them closely. How do they think in different situations? When are they in a good mood, how do they like to communicate? Try not to tick them off. You may even have to go to extremes to connect with them. Come in earlier for work than everyone else and catch them alone one morning or stay later than others if you have to. Also, be prepared when you do get their time. Don't waste it.

3. **Cover Weaknesses** – great leaders learn how to step up when something isn't getting done. When you work for a bad boss, there will be ample opportunities for you to step up and fill the gap. By that, I mean you can take ownership of something that is not getting done. In doing so, you will develop some skills you didn't have, and you gain perspective and experience about an area you may not have known much about. You cover your boss' weaknesses and make them look good. I am not suggesting you turn a blind eye to harm's way. If there is something not being done that is putting lives at risk, you have to report it. However, if you see something in your area that is not being done at all or is lacking excellence, step up and do it. Don't wait for someone to tell you to do it. You may be viewed as crazy when you do, but when your time comes to get a better job or be promoted, it will be all worth it. Sometimes, to get what others don't have, you have to do what others won't do. Step up.

4. **Problem Solving** – bad bosses typically make bad decisions, and bad decisions come with problems. Similar to covering weaknesses, working for a bad boss will teach you how to manage and solve problems. Realize some problems cannot be solved, they have to be managed. Learning to keep things in perspective and dealing with problems will make you a better leader. Every leader carries two buckets in their hands; one with gas and the other with water. Problems in the workplace, like a fire, can get bigger or smaller depending which bucket you use. Minimizing damage and controlling problems is a skill that will serve you well for years to come.

5. **Mental Toughness** – perspective is half the battle. A horrible boss is not usually the best communicator, and they can come off demanding, oppressive, and cold. While I would never advocate subjecting yourself to an abusive work environment, or relationship, there is a difference between a tough boss and a horrible boss. There are many leaders that are very demanding and tough, and if you are a person who is overly sensitive and easily offended, being under a tough boss may be good for you. Sometimes we really do need to grow thicker skin as we develop. I guarantee you will encounter a coarse leader or boss. Becoming more "mentally tough" or less sensitive will make you a better leader.

Not all bad things are completely bad in and of themselves. We always have a part to play in how we choose to respond to every situation, especially challenging ones. Working with a horrible boss can and will be one of the greatest seasons of growth you can endure. The worst thing you could do is run from a hard situation that would actually be great "training ground" for you. If you can change your perspective and see the positives you can glean from a poor leader or boss, you will be stronger, more mature, and better equipped to lead in the future.

CHAPTER 8

MISTAKES AND MESS UPS

*"The only real mistake is
the one from which we learn nothing."*

—

HENRY FORD

Not Dealing with Problems

Growing up in the country, we lived far enough out that we were not connected to the city sewage. All our waste went into a large tank buried in the ground far from our house. I never even knew it existed until one day I knew we had a bad problem. I had finished doing the dishes in the kitchen and suddenly water started coming back up the drain into the sink. At first, I thought it was clogged because I was notorious for trying to wash food or remnants too big for the pipes. After several tries to fix the problem, it wasn't getting any better and now it seemed even more water had backed up into the drain.

At this point, I had to let my dad know. You always knew at our house when a problem had worsened enough that you had to let dad know. Immediately, he came and looked at it and said, "Septic tank is full!".

"Huh?" I said. "What is a septic tank?" My dad explained to me the waste storage tank in the ground that catches all of our water from the house. Dad being dad then mentioned it was very expensive to fix because you had to hire a truck to come out, break open the ground and pump all the waste into a tanker and haul it away. Seemed simple enough except we couldn't afford it.

My dad was coming back from a severe car accident and couldn't work as much so we didn't have the money to fix it. He had put off fixing the sewage tank by limiting what areas of the house we would use water in. It worked for a while but after several weeks the problem worsened, and water was starting to back up into our bathrooms. Something had to be done or it would eventually spill over onto our floors. Enter MacGyver! My dad somehow came up with the brilliant idea we could rent a sewage pump on our own and pump the sewage into a field nearby and drain our tank saving us tons of money since we were so broke. Since I was the only other male in the house, I volunteered to help my dad with this horrible job. I will never forget that day for as long as I live.

I will spare the details here, but I can tell you when we dug up the ground and opened that sewage tank, I almost fainted. It was so gross. My dad ran in the other direction gagging and spitting from the putrid smell he couldn't escape. After he gathered himself, he took the pump and lowered it into the sea of grossness and began pumping out the sewage. This took many hours with bouts of my dad pulling out the pump regularly to clean off the screen around it. To say I am still scarred from this is an understatement. We eventually got the sewage all out and thankfully we lived far enough away from the city and other people we didn't go to jail for what we did. Nobody could see or smell the mess. From that day forward our house was operable again. Life resumed to normal with showers, clean dishes, bathroom usage, and lots of laundry getting done that had backed up.

I share that story with you because as leaders, we may not have to deal with sewage in a septic tank, but we will have to deal with problems. Sometimes the problems are big, nasty, and hard to solve. Leadership and problem solving go hand in hand. You get both once you sign up. You don't get to choose one or the other. Where things go wrong for us as leaders is often we don't want to deal with problems. We put them off and procrastinate. We delay or ignore the problem hoping it will go away. But guess what, problems don't ever go away on their own. You need to solve them. The longer you put off dealing with problems, the bigger they will get and sometimes even become more complex. <u>As we get into this topic, let's look at five messes that can potentially happen if we fail to deal with problems.</u>

1. **The Problem Will Grow Larger** – if you refuse to deal with a problem, you are currently having, rest assured it will get bigger over time. I recall having an issue with one of our employees because this individual wouldn't do the little things I asked of him. At first, I thought it wasn't a big deal. I never addressed it and the problem got bigger because he started ignoring other, bigger things. I asked him and other staff asked him. I kept letting it go hoping he would turn it around at some point but he never did and the other staff started complaining to me about him because he wouldn't listen to them either. Eventually the problem escalated to a blow up that caused me lots of extra work, pain, and difficulty in the years ahead. If I would have dealt with it from the start, I would have saved myself so much trouble.

2. **Staff Morale Will Decline** – looking back at the problem we had in my house growing up, I now see how much it was negatively impacting everyone living there. No showers, laundry backing up, dishes dirty, and high stress levels took its toll on us. As a leader, whenever you have problems, others are looking to you for answers and direction. What is going on? What do we do? How do we fix it?

How long will it take? You may not always hear these questions directly but trust me, they are being asked and discussed. The longer the problem exists, the more it will wear on people. The more the problem grows; the more morale will decline. Problems in general just have that kind of effect. Whenever you have a problem, work to see the bigger picture and the potential negative ways it can weigh on your staff and department. At times you may not have anything you can do about it, but just by acknowledging it and letting others know you are aware of it allows them to vent and give you a perspective on how bad it is.

3. **You Will Lose Respect** – one of the worst things I have seen happen is a leader losing respect because they refuse to confront or deal with a problem. No matter what the reason is for avoiding it, this is a dangerous place. If you begin to lose respect for those you are leading, your influence will diminish over time. People may be nice to you in person, but inwardly they have lost respect and will not follow you. Respect is the currency for influence. The higher the respect of those you lead, the more you can motivate them and influence them one way or the other. The less respect you have, the harder it will be to get anything done.

4. **You Will Not Get Promoted** – problem solvers get promoted. Period. Not dealing with problems will keep you stuck or eventually get you demoted. By not dealing with hard situations, you will harm your career path. In fact, most, if not all, interviews for bigger jobs and roles usually have several questions that deal with how you would handle or manage problems. Not only do they want to ask you questions about problem solving, but they will also want you to share examples of problems you have solved in the past. If you want to move up as a leader, you must learn to deal with problems. Your future depends on it.

5. **The Problem Gets More Complex** – could you have imagined what would have happened if my dad didn't come up with a solution to fix our septic tank? Not only would our floors have been ruined, but eventually we would have had to move out because of bacteria and the risk of getting very sick. The problem, though simple at the time, would have become very complex quickly. Leaders face the same danger. Not dealing with an employee's tardiness or a habit of not following through on a project can cause your department to not be relied upon. If you are not reliable, others will find a way to avoid working with you as much as they can, causing strain in another department. Now the problem has become cancerous and infiltrated other areas and other staff. The more layers a problem has, the more potential it has to gain complexity. Problems are already hard to deal with and keeping them from becoming complex is critical to your leadership and your ability to solve them. I encourage you to adjust your perspective and attitude when dealing with problems. If this is something you really have struggled with in the past, get some coaching and mentorship in this area. Problem solving is a skill you can improve over time. I remember the story of a ship repairman that was called to fix one of the engines on a boat. The man they brought in had been fixing ship engines since he was young. Once he arrived, the owner of the boat watched closely to see what he would do. Immediately the repairman went to work, and examined the engine top to bottom. After some time, he reached into his bag and pulled out a hammer. He gently tapped on an area of the engine and it came back to life. Afterwards, the owner received the invoice. The invoice read: $10,000.00. Outraged, the owner of the ship asked him why it was so much when he didn't do much to fix the problem. The repairman said, "The labor of tapping with the hammer only cost $2.00, but knowing where to tap cost $9,998.00."[27] Knowing how to solve problems will do the same for

you as well. Maybe not $10,000 dollars' worth, but ultimately it will pay dividends to you as a leader.

Pressure Magnifies

Have you ever witnessed what intense heat and pressure can do? I have and I will never forget it. One summer when we went on a Griswold-like family vacation to Disneyland in Florida, we were sitting in our station wagon at a stop light waiting for the light to change. Suddenly, there was this loud bang of a noise, and the hood on the station wagon popped open, completely blocking the view of the window. It was like someone turned out the lights. I remember being so confused and wondering why the sun had gone away. My dad said something under his breath, hopped out the car to stare at the hissing, steaming engine. Being the curious boy I was, I got out of the car and walked up beside my dad and said, "What is it?" Immediately, he answered back. "It's the radiator. The car overheated." My next question to my dad was genius. "What do we do now?" I have never forgotten what happens if you let a car overheat. The engine has the potential to blow if left unmonitored. It can cause irreparable damage to your car, and could harm you.

Pressure magnifies. As a leader you will deal with pressure. You cannot avoid, run from it, delegate it, or dumb it down. Pressure magnifies. Who you are on the inside is clearly seen and known the most by others when you go through difficult times. It isn't when things are going well, it is when the bottom falls out, and you feel the heat; and everyone sees it. Ignoring it or passing it off as no big deal over time is a weakness that will limit or stall your growth as a leader.

My dad eventually got us back up and running. We took the car to the shop and replaced a hose that was leaking fluid, and causing the car to overheat. Once the hose was replaced and the lost fluid was restored, the car ran great again and we didn't have any more issues. Leadership is much the same. What is the root issue causing the pressure? Are there any weaknesses in your character that need to be addressed to avoid a blow up? Let's look at five ways we respond to intense pressure and some possible pitfalls of each.

1. **Anger** – are you someone who gets angry easily? Are you the type of person who snaps and goes off? Is there some kind of betrayal, injustice, or hurt you have been carrying around from your past? Have you been dealing with levels of built up frustration from your work or home life? If so, your response to pressure will be like walking through a field of landmines. Explosive anger can cause damage you may not be able to come back from.

2. **Control** – leaders who respond to pressure with paranoia and fear often resort to control. Typically, wherever you find very controlling leaders, you find low morale. Those who resort to controlling others lose their identity, purpose, and creativity. They will do only what you want, so that you calm down and leave them alone. Control is an over inflated sense of what one brings to the table. If they don't do it, then it won't be done right. Nobody can lead as well as they do. Ego is in the driver seat and insecurity is in the back seat. As a leader, your goal should be pulling people through teaching and coaching, not pushing them through correction and control .

3. **Manipulate** – great leaders don't manipulate, they motivate. Control and manipulation are good friends. Leaders are responsible for getting things done. Manipulation works, but it leaves carnage in its wake. The loss of trust and confidence can be so severe you never earn it back. No matter how effective manipulation may seem, it is never worth it. Character and integrity are the bedrock of every leader's style and approach no matter how they lead. If people know you have their best interests at heart and that you are looking out for them, the loyalty and trust will go a long way for you.

4. **Isolate** – when the pressure is on, some leaders seem to disappear. They retreat, run, and hide. By not deciding, they have decided. To do nothing. To check out. Pressure and stress can be debilitating to a leader in many ways. Isolation creates more pressure because avoidance solves nothing. Disappearing may feel like the answer, but addressing whatever is causing the pressure and alleviating it will pay off more positively. Isolating yourself will only make you even more reactive.

5. **Medicate** – some leaders, when paralyzed by pressure, medicate. Drinking, drugs, or other forms of addiction can deteriorate health and reputation. Dealing with pressure is stressful but medicating or numbing against stress can ruin lives. I have witnessed the damaging effects of numbing the pain of whatever difficulty you are going through. Do not compromise. Do not impede your decision-making ability. Guard and protect your character and integrity at all costs. No drink, drug, or poor lifestyle habit is worth you blowing your reputation and hurting your family or those you work with. You may experience some of these responses at some point. While it does not disqualify you from leadership, it does mean you need to be self-aware and proactive. When we are aware of chinks in the armor, and we keep plodding along up the career ladder thinking we can manage them, our unwillingness to address them will only lead to collapse and destruction.

Years ago, a friend of mine in college had some habits that weren't conducive for leading a family and holding a very high position at an institution that demanded significant moral character. He lived one way in front of the public and his family, and a totally different way while away on trips and private events. Those habits followed him and eventually caught up to him. Moral failing when you are twenty-one is perhaps understandable, but when you have a family and lead a state institution

MISTAKES AND MESS UPS

of high character, the ramifications are devastating. Remember this: the higher your climb on the corporate ladder, the stronger your character must be.

Learning From Your Mistakes

I hate falling. I'm a big guy, I'm not very graceful and falling hurts. The inevitable laughter from any witnesses to my fall does not help matters. One of the most terrifying falls occurred when I was in eighth grade. I had broken my right leg playing football and was stuck in a cast that went from my toes all the way to the top of my thigh. Back then a full body cast was basically the answer to anything broken. Doctors wanted to immobilize you as much as possible to help the limb heal.

The fall occurred one evening as I was laying on my bed relaxing after dinner. My step mom called me to come get some chocolate cake for dessert. I don't waste time when dessert is on the line. I jumped off the bed, grabbed my crutches, and hustled to the top of the staircase. In my urgency to head down the stairs, I forgot which goes first: crutches or feet. I put my foot down first and the crutches catapulted me into the air, my feet dangling above me. My arms were trapped by the handles of the crutches. I was heading face-first down the stairs with no way of stopping. Thankfully, I had the presence of mind to flip around and land on my backside instead of my face. It was over as soon as it started. I slid butt-first all the way to the bottom, hitting each step on the way down.

Upon landing, I pretended nothing was wrong. My family was watching television directly in front of the staircase, and they all leapt to their feet with their mouths open in horror. I reassured them I was alright, even though I was not. I was in pain and more than a little embarrassed. The athlete of the family didn't know how to use crutches. As bad as I hurt, my pride would not let me show any emotion or concern. I learned a valuable lesson from that fall. Besides never forgetting how to use crutches properly on the stairs, I learned everyone makes mistakes and everyone falls down occasionally. It doesn't matter how smart, strong, athletic, successful, or independent we are, we will make mistakes.

As you venture into leadership, keep this in mind: You are going to make mistakes along the way. Failure is part of the process. When this happens to you, there are two choices you will be faced with in regards to your mistakes:

A. You can learn from it.

B. You can run from it.

When I talk about learning from your mistakes, I am speaking of a process that takes time. If you have ever touched a hot stove, you felt the sting of pain from the heat. You got burned. It hurt for days after and left a mark; depending on how bad the burn was you may have had to bandage it. The skin was damaged and it took time to heal. From that moment on, whenever you see a stove you cautiously check it before touching it. You don't avoid stoves, but you learned a valuable lesson from getting burned. On the other hand, people who continually make the same mistakes over and over again never seem to learn. They run from their mistakes, always get bailed out. Once a mistake is made, they either blame someone else or find an easy way out. They refuse to take responsibility for their failures. They look for a way to either avoid the consequences or find someone to get them off the hook. The problem with those who do this when making a mistake is that they never really learn anything. If you never learn from your mistakes, then you never change for the better. As a leader, some of the best lessons you will ever learn will be painful. Like that hot stove, if you never felt some level of pain you would cause more damage to yourself by not removing your hand. Benjamin Franklin said, "That which hurts, also instructs."[28] If you never feel the pain of making a mistake, you run the risk of forming a habit of making mistakes. The more you make the same mistakes, the more it becomes a habit. The higher you move up in your career you will have more at stake and the more people your mistakes will impact. Learn from your mistakes early on, don't run from them. The more you slow down, reflect and learn from your mistakes, the greater wisdom you gain. As you move into bigger roles of influence it will serve you well.

One of the biggest mistakes of my career happened early on at the University of Texas. I had just accepted an incredible opportunity working under football strength coach, Jeff "Maddog" Madden. As a young coach, I thought I knew it all. Anyone who didn't agree with my philosophy of training was wrong, in my opinion. We were using some unorthodox methods of training I had never used and didn't really believe in at the time. One day after a session, one of the offensive lineman was complaining about what we were doing. He turned to me and asked, "Why are we doing this?" With a critical and judgmental spirit I replied, "I don't know. This isn't the best way to get you in shape anyway." A few weeks later, my flippant comment reached Coach Mack Brown as evidence someone was smack-talking the strength program. Coach Brown called a meeting with all strength staff that day to get to the bottom of the issue. He gathered us into a room, and asked each one of us if we had spoken out against the program. I confessed my wrong doing, and owned up to what I had said.

After the meeting I met with my boss. I don't remember exactly what he said that day but he was yelling, upset, and pounding his fists on his desk. I had my computer privileges revoked and I was fearful of losing my job moving forward. I was on thin ice, having broken trust with my coworkers and I lost credibility. I humbled myself and went back to work. I became a team player and changed my attitude. I could have quit, walked away, and become a victim, without learning a thing. I made the choice to stay. It took me two years to get out of the hole I dug for myself but gradually I earned back the trust and credibility I had lost. Day after day, month after month, I chose to use my mistakes to help me mature and grow up as a leader. That one failure ended up being a turning point in my leadership career, as several years later I was promoted to top assistant. By staying the course and enduring the pain of learning from my mistake, I developed skills to be a more humble coach and leader.

Today it seems everyone wants to move up quick and fast. How do I get to your position? The reality is, it takes time and a big part of the process is making and learning from your mistakes. I have seen too many younger leaders today who do not learn from their mistakes. They blame-shift, walk in denial, and avoid the consequences at all cost. Let's look at five potential outcomes if we don't learn from our mistakes:

1. **Repeat Mistakes** – if there is one thing that can damage your leadership is repeating the same mistakes. Making mistakes occasionally can hurt you but you can recover from them. Making the same mistakes over and over again can ruin you. One way to evaluate this is to look at your track record. Are there any patterns that stand out to you? Do you seem to get stuck in a rut at times? Do you ever take time out to reflect on how the problem happened in the first place? If not, I encourage you the next time you make a mistake, stop and analyze it. Do an "autopsy" on it. Really seek to get to the root of why it happened.

2. **Improperly Handling Criticism** – whenever you make a mistake, criticism is likely right around the corner. Sometimes it can be constructive and helpful, and other times it can be personal and destructive. It can tear you down. Like touching the hot stove, be careful you don't completely avoid the sting of criticism. One word of advice to help with this is always consider the source it comes from. Is that person trustworthy? Do they have a tendency to be harsh? Do they have your best interest in mind? When someone is critical of you, all of it may not be warranted but I have found if you don't take it personally and get defensive, there is always a grain of truth in it to help you improve.

3. **Loss of Compassion and Empathy** – the greatest way you learn and develop compassion and empathy is going through something painful yourself. For years, I had severe lower back pain and had times where I would struggle to even walk. Guess what kind of people I have a ton of compassion for? Anyone who suffers from back pain. I know how it feels and how debilitating it can be. I am quick to offer a word of encouragement, help them stand up, or refer them to a doctor I know can help. In a similar way, when you refuse to learn from your mistakes you run the risk of not developing compassion. Compassion or empathy is a skill all great leaders display. They feel the pain of those under their care. Tyrants lack compassion and run over people, leading from a place of fear not love. In their eyes they never make mistakes and own up to them. To do so is soft and showing weakness.

4. **Loss of Better Opportunities** – leadership is all about solving and dealing with problems. The better you learn how to deal with and manage problems the more opportunities you will get. The bigger the opportunity, the larger the problems you will encounter. The bigger the problem, the better the leadership needed to solve the problem. The only way to improve at problem solving is by making mistakes and learning from them. If you continually fail to learn from your mistakes, over time you run the risk of not being considered for bigger roles. Any and every mistake you make, be sure to view it as an opportunity to get stronger. In doing so, you will increase your chances of getting bigger opportunities to lead.

5. **Loss of Relatability** – have you ever been around or worked with a leader who never makes a mistake? They almost seem inhuman. These types of leaders are very hard to connect with and relate to. They always seem to have their guard up. Somewhere along the way they bought into the lie that being a leader means you never can

make a mistake. The truth is, though, people relate to your mistakes more than they do your successes. That is the human side of leadership. It makes you more relatable. It will be your failures, flops, and fumbles that help you influence others and earn their respect more than anything. When we fail to own up to our mistakes, learn from them and be vulnerable, it turns people off. We become inhuman and lose touch with our people. When you make a mistake, don't be too proud to admit it. You don't have to dwell on it but minimally acknowledge it. Letting others know when you mess up makes you more attractive as a leader. It draws them closer to you and your influence will increase.

A word of caution when it comes to making mistakes and learning from them. Do not personalize your mistakes. Failing does not make you a failure. Messing up may sting but do not let it make you feel inferior. It's ok to have a bad day, but don't let it turn into a bad life. When I fell down the steps on my crutches, I didn't stay down. I popped right back up and after I settled down from the shock of it, I went into the kitchen and ate my cake. My leg was in pain and hurt for many days after that but I never made that mistake again. I learned from it and got better. When you make a mistake, pick yourself back up, dust yourself off and learn from it. Don't disqualify yourself. Don't be too hard on yourself. There are many lessons we need to learn on this journey of leadership. Each lesson is valuable and necessary. Keep the big picture in mind. Besides, whoever said you can't 'have your cake and eat it too' was off. You can have your cake and eat too, because in the end you will have earned your cake as you fail your way into success.

The 7 Most Powerful Words

Have you ever had one of those days where you mess up? Not only do you mess up, you do it to one of your co-workers. Sometimes, being in a position of leadership can give you a false sense of power or superiority and, without always realizing it, you start treating others poorly. One night, some teams were coming in to train late and I didn't care too much for the music that was playing. Without asking, I changed the music to what I wanted, not considering if anyone else was listening or had a preference. One of our staff, who was also in the weight room working with some athletes, came up and mentioned that they were listening to that station. In all my glory, I snapped back something along the lines of "I'm not changing the music – we are listening to this station now." To say I power tripped is an understatement. I thought to myself, "I'm tired, it's late, and I am in charge". Immediately, I felt the sting in my conscience. First of all, the staff member who I treated so poorly was a great guy. He would have totally gone along with a change of music if I asked nicely. To make matters worse, I avoided him over the next hour and had intentions to slip out the back door unnoticed and head home. My conscience yelling even louder now would not ease up. *That's it*, I decided. *I can't take it anymore. I need to apologize to him.* For the next ten minutes, I wrestled back and forth if I should say anything to him. On one shoulder, the little devil spoke into my ear, "You are in charge and don't need to apologize. He should do what you say and that's that." Then the little angel spoke to me from my other shoulder, "You are the leader, and he is your friend and colleague. You have to apologize."

I went up to him and asked to meet with him. He agreed and, as we entered the office and closed the door, you could see he was ready for a fight. His guard was up and his body language was sending messages of defense and protection. I paused for a moment to collect my thoughts then said, "I want to say first and foremost, I was wrong how I treated you just now. I shouldn't have spoken to you like that. I am sorry, will you forgive me?" The look on his face was shocking to me. His mouth was open with a look of shock and amazement. Immediately, I saw his guard drop as his features softened. After a few moments of silence, he spoke and said "It's no big deal. I appreciate you saying that. We can listen to whatever station tonight." For the rest of that night, I cannot recall what happened, except for one thing. Our relationship improved from that encounter. Looking back, I learned such a valuable lesson in leadership and life. When you mess up, own it and apologize for what you did. Saying you are sorry and genuinely meaning it is so powerful. They are truly the seven most powerful words a leader can say. Let's take a look at five principles of apologies that will help you lead others better.

1. **Don't Delay** – it's never too late to say you are sorry, however once you commit an offense the sooner you apologize for it, the more impact it can have. Sometimes waiting to say you are sorry can cause more damage. There will be times to wait to apologize, but generally speaking it's better to not put it off.

2. **Be Genuine** – when you apologize, there should be a tone of remorse and regret for what you have done. If you apologize flippantly without any remorse, it can actually make matters much worse. Not only is timing important for saying you're sorry, so is tone. Part of making things right with someone is feeling the hurt you've caused. It shows you genuinely care.

3. **Be Specific** – when you do sit down to say you are sorry, it is imperative you specifically say what it was you did wrong. As a leader, realizing your shortcomings and naming the offense you caused shows a human side of vulnerability to those you are leading that can actually earn you more credibility and trust with them. Not apologizing or admitting what you did that was wrong, can be seen as arrogant or prideful. This can have the opposite effect of saying you are sorry. It can make you repulsive.

4. **Don't Justify Your Wrongs** – this might be the most important principle for apologizing. If, in any way, shape or form you even hint at justifying your wrongful actions, it is *not* and I repeat, it is *not* an

apology. It's an excuse and you are trying to get off the hook. Own what you did, call it out, and apologize for it. Practically speaking, this can be one of the hardest things to do because leaders like to be seen in a position of power and leverage. When you apologize, you place yourself willingly in a position of vulnerability with those you are leading. After you admit your wrong, be quiet and wait for the other person's response. Most of the time, if you handle it right it will be a favorable response. A word of caution here though. There will be times you don't get a good response from the other person. That is ok. You are apologizing not to get a reaction from them but to clean up the mess you made. When, if and how they respond is up to them. Going into a meeting to apologize expecting a certain response can set you up for failure. Do your part and own it, say you are sorry but don't under any circumstance try to dictate how someone should respond. Hopefully they will receive it with grace and compassion, and forgive you but if they don't that is ok. Take the high road.

5. **Change Your Behavior** – once you apologize, the next step is where the rubber meets the road. Whatever action it was you did wrong, really make an effort to change and improve in that area. By doing so, you are sending a message you really care about the individual. Apologizing over and over again for the same thing again and again will cause others not to trust you or believe you. Your apology will have no weight to it. Your credibility will drop immensely and leading others will become very difficult. By changing your behavior, it gives others hope that you are paying attention and that the workplace environment and relationships matter to you as a leader. It has the potential to influence and change behaviors in those who are following and watching you. Remember it's not what we say that

has the most power, it's what we do that will influence others the most and make the biggest impact over time.

As we wrap this chapter up, take a moment and reflect on your leadership. Is there anything you have done wrong or anyone you have mistreated that you need to apologize for or to? It may not even be something big to you but that doesn't make it right to ignore it or brush it off. Even a small leak in a house over time can completely ruin it so you cannot live in it. The smallest offenses have the ability to add up over time and cause great damage if left unchecked. Are there any areas of pride or superiority in your leadership? Do you talk down to others, power trip and treat them less than just because they are underneath you? The way you treat and talk to others can be a gauge on how prideful you are or how you have overestimated your own sense of worth. Dealing with this attitude will be a must before you can begin to see any wrongs you have committed. The most slippery slope for a leader is to have a lot of power and wield it whenever they want thinking there won't be a consequence for it. Understand this, just because you can, doesn't mean you should. The best leaders know they have power but they use it only when they need to. Usually it's to help others rather than hurt them. The better we become at realizing when we are wrong and apologizing for it will give us power not take it away. Remember that as you use the seven most powerful words with others!

LEADERSHIP NAVIGATION: *LINING IT ALL UP*

"The pessimist complains about the wind.
The optimist expects it to change.
The leader adjusts the sails."

—

WILLIAM ARTHUR WARD

When a ship gets close to a harbor and is seeking to dock, a narrow, shallow channel can be dangerous and risky territory to run aground, especially if visibility is poor. To help signal to the captain that the ship is aligned safely in the deepest and widest part of the canal, there are two lights positioned on land. These lights are commonly referred to as leading lights, and they act as beacons to create a line for the ships to guide them safely into the harbor.[29] Positionally, one light is placed further and higher in elevation than the other light. As a ship gets closer to the harbor, the lights must be aligned vertically to ensure safe entry. If the lights are not aligned correctly, the ship could run aground, causing damage to the ship and taking on water.

In a similar way, we have covered eight different leadership lights that will aid you in your leadership journey. Just like a ship entering a harbor carries goods, wares, and priceless items to help those on land, so your leadership will help others along the way as you line up the different aspects of your leadership. Neglecting or ignoring any one of these guiding lights could be detrimental to your development as well as to those you lead and influence. The captain of a ship looks to line up the lights to aid their navigation and safe positioning in the water, and the different aspects of leadership will help you navigate the different seasons of your leadership journey as well. As we conclude, let's review:

Attitude – every leader's attitude will have a direct influence on their ability to move up no matter what place or position they hold. There is no excuse for having a bad attitude as a leader. The greatest leaders will face difficulties, hardships and unfair treatment like the rest of us, but their attitude will help guide them in these seasons.

Mentality – how you think and see situations as a leader has the power to change your outcomes. If there is one difference that separates leaders and the varying outcomes they get, it is their ability to think. No two leaders think the same. How you think will determine how you lead. How you lead can determine if you win or lose. Mentality matters.

Professionalism – professionalism has nothing to do with the job you have, but rather how you do your job. Two leaders can hold the same job with similar responsibilities and be perceived differently. What is the difference? Professionalism. How you dress, talk, walk, treat people, communicate, and carry yourself can elevate you or bring you down.

Authenticity – the best leaders aren't perfect. They don't always have to be right, but they do always keep it real. Today, more than ever people are eagerly searching for genuine, sincere, and authentic leadership to get behind and follow. Being vulnerable, approachable and taking off the armor not only makes you more attractive, it demonstrates strength under control. When you focus on being yourself and not trying to copy another person, your influence will increase.

Competence – authenticity is powerful, but at the end of the day, you must still be good at what you do. Just because people like you, doesn't always mean they will follow you. When a leader is competent, they gain confidence and commitment from their followers. People want to follow you because you get results. If you are not competent at what you do, respect and trust are lost over time. Lose those and eventually your leadership capital will bankrupt.

Career Stallers and Stoppers – if there is one area where leaders must be tuned in, it is to where they are lacking. If a leader continues to run into a wall that keeps them from advancing or moving up, intervention may be needed. Failing to address weakness in character or bad habits can be a barrier to growth and promotion. Humble yourself, seek feedback, and take ownership of any areas you see blocking you. Any weak spot you refuse to confront will never change.

Personal Development – growth is a choice. The best leaders realize this and are intentionally creative about it. Like a wise master builder, the best leaders invest in themselves. They make time to expand and increase themselves. They are continually seeking to improve and level up their leadership. Even if they must endure a season under a bad boss, they use it to their advantage. Personal growth and development has no room for making excuses. Every obstacle has the seed of potential to become an opportunity. Use it or lose it.

Mistakes and Mess Ups – everyone makes mistakes, especially leaders. Mistakes are expected, but should not be left unaddressed. Not dealing with problems can become a problem. In your leadership journey, develop the habit of facing your problems head on. It won't always be fun and comfortable, but it will be a garden for growth. Pressure will increase and you will get exposed, but if you embrace it and learn from it, what was once a weakness can become a strength. There is nothing wrong with starting out small as a leader, just don't stay that way. When you do make mistakes that impact others negatively, be sure to apologize. Not admitting and owning up to your mistakes ultimately is avoiding responsibility. Refuse to be a leader who only is comfortable when praise is being handed out. Be the same person no matter the outcome. Own it if you do great, and own it if you mess up. With the right perspective ultimately you never really lose, you will learn and grow.

It has been many years since that alarm went off at 4:30 am and I sat on the edge of my boss's guest bed. Seasons have come and seasons have gone. Now, more than ever, I realize the importance of leadership. I may not be where I want to be, but I am not where I used to be. My journey has been filled with ups and downs, setbacks and set ups, heroes and heartbreaks. Your journey will be the same.

Every person can learn to lead. Leadership isn't just for a select few elite folks. Some are more gifted to lead than others, but everyone can learn leadership. How you apply these nuances of leadership will be your secret sauce. If you are diligent to learn and apply these areas in your leadership, like the leading lights ships use entering the harbor to stay and arrive at their destination, you too will find success. Strong leadership is needed more than ever today. The world needs more leaders who are authentic, humble, competent and passionate. The world needs you. Stand out and be set apart. Find your secret sauce and be the difference maker you were meant to be.

ENDNOTES

1   Podcast, The John Maxwell Leadership, et al. *John Maxwell Leadership Podcast*, 17 Apr. 2019, johnmaxwellleadershippodcast.com/ episodes/john-maxwell-your-influence-inventory#:~:text=John%20 C.,you%27re%20a%20good%20leader.

2   Kroc , Ray. Ray Kroc - *When You're Green, Your Growing. When You're... - Brainyquote*, www.brainyquote.com/quotes/ray_kroc_106051. Accessed 11 Aug. 2023.

3   Chand, Samuel R. *Leadership Pain: The Classroom for Growth*. Thomas Nelson, 2015.

4   "Face the Storm." CrossFit Amundson, crossfitamundson.com/ coachescorner/face-the-storm/. Accessed 11 Aug. 2023.

5   https://www.merriam-webster.com/dictionary/disposition

6   "Robert Ludlum Quote: 'Blessed Are the Flexible for They Will Not Allow Themselves to Become Bent out of Shape!'" *Quotefancy,* quotefancy. com/quote/1303775/Robert-Ludlum-Blessed-are-the-flexible-for-they-will-not-allow-themselves-to-become-bent. Accessed 11 Aug. 2023.

7   https://alabamanewscenter.com/2019/12/02/ on-this-day-in-1972-the-earth-opened-up-underneath-calera-ala/

8   "The 2 Kinds of People: Cam Taylor." *Cam Taylor | Be Inspired. Be Focused. Be Tenacious.*, 15 Nov. 2012, camtaylor.net/2012/11/15/the-2-kinds-of-people/.

9 https://www.merriam-webster.com/dictionary/professional

10 Maxwell, John C. "The Position Myth ." *The 360 -Degree Leader: Developing Your Influence from Anywhere in the Organization*, Thomas Nelson, Nashville, 2011, pp. 4–7.

11 Maxwell, John C. *Winning with People: Discover the People Principles That Work for You Every Time.* HarperCollins Leadership, 2007.

12 https://en.wikipedia.org/wiki/Personal_branding

13 Newport, C. (2020). *Digital Minimalism.* Penguin Books Ltd.

14 https://www.thoughtco.com/possible-origins-of-sincere-and-sincerely-118268#:~:text=The%20origin%20of%20the%20word,from%20Latin%20for%20%27without%20wax.

15 https://www.biblegateway.com/passage/?search=James+1%3A6-8&version=NIV

16 https://www.pinterest.com/pin/2181499806787299/?nic_v2=1a3f0IT7g

17 *Bruce Lee quote: "Empty your cup so that it may be filled; become devoid to gain totality."* Quotefancy. (n.d.-a). https://quotefancy.com/quote/25974/Bruce-Lee-Empty-your-cup-so-that-it-may-be-filled-become-devoid-to-gain-totality

18 https://twitter.com/robertmadu/status/771484612484792321?lang=en#:~:text=%40robertmadu-,Pride%20is%20like%20bad%20breath%3A%20everyone,you%20have%20it%20but%20you.

19 https://en.wikipedia.org/wiki/Icarus

20 Proverbs 11:2 NIV — bible gateway. (n.d.). https://www.biblegateway.com/passage/?search=Proverbs%2B11%3A2&version=NIV

21 https://graciousquotes.com/humility/

22 People would rather be electrically shocked than left alone
with their ... (n.d.-a). https://www.science.org/content/article/
people-would-rather-be-electrically-shocked-left-alone-their-thoughts

23 *Tony Dungy quote: "courage is the ability to do the right thing, all the
time, no matter how painful or uncomfortable it might be."* Quotefancy.
(n.d.-f).
https://quotefancy.com/quote/1169127/Tony-Dungy-Courage-is-the-
ability-to-do-the-right-thing-all-the-time-no-matter-how

24 Admin. (2018, March 26). *Art consulting firm thinks outside the box.*
Modern In Denver-Colorado's Design Magazine.
https://www.modernindenver.com/2015/01/outside-the-box/

25 Epstein, D. (2020). Range. Pan Macmillan.

26 Tice, L. E., & Quick, J. (2004). *Personal coaching for results: How
to mentor and inspire others to amazing growth.* Thomas Nelson
Publishers, a division of Thomas Nelson, Inc.

27 Cole, N. (2023, July 17). The ship repair man story.
Medium. https://medium.com/@oceanbcreative/
the-ship-repair-man-story-dd959a4469d8

28 *Benjamin Franklin quote: "That which hurts, also instructs."*
Quotefancy. (n.d.-a). https://quotefancy.com/quote/772113/
Benjamin-Franklin-That-which-hurts-also-instructs

29 https://en.wikipedia.org/wiki/Leading_lights

ACKNOWLEDGMENTS

I would like to start off by thanking and honoring my dad and mom. Though they are no longer with me, their love, support, and guidance through the years helped me grow up and be the best husband and father I could be.

I would also like to thank all of the mentors, coaches, and athletes through the years I have had the privilege of learning from and working with. Without them, I wouldn't have made it this far and learned all the valuable lessons that have sustained me in my career. I stand upon your shoulders.

Specifically, at the University of Texas there have been so many people I am grateful for. Coach Mack Brown and Jeff "Maddog" Madden for hiring me in 1998, DeLoss Dodds and Chris Plonsky for their leadership, support, example and encouragement, Chris Del Conte who has taught me no goal is too big, Coach Jerritt Elliott who taught me that good people love people, Coach Michael Center who has taught me how to re-build your life when it comes crashing down, Coach Bruce Berque who has taught me the importance of details and organization to be successful, and Allen "Godfather" Hardin who has been in my corner from day one encouraging me and helping grow as a leader.

I would also like to say a special thanks to all the staff I have had the privilege of working alongside with and serving through the years at Texas. Sandy Abney, Trey Zepeda, Anna Craig, Melissa Schmtiz, Clint

Martin, Michael Hanson, Joe Krawczyk, Matt Couch, Nic Higgins, Jesse Ackerman, Tim Cross, Derrick Scott, Chuck Faucette, Jeff Earls, Angel Spassov, Lee McCormick, Stephen Whalen, Lance Sewell, Beth Byron, and Brent Metz. Thank you for all the memories, lessons, and support.

I would also like to specially thank some mentors who have significantly impacted my life and career trajectory. Coach Steve Duke, my high school offensive line coach who pushed me to greatness and to this day still calls me "stud".E. J. "Doc" Kreis who sadly passed away recently but if it weren't for him, I wouldn't be where I am today as a coach and leader. Thank you Doc! He not only coached me in his free time when I was struggling as a college athlete at Georgia, he gave me my first job to coach at the University of Colorado when I had no idea of what my career would be. Dave Plettl, a true friend, mentor, and colleague that has always been a great example of what it means to coach with excellence and not neglect your family along the way. Coach Dan Pfaff, who was the first coach and mentor to teach how to analyze the body and movement from a global perspective. To Jim Tindall, my karate instructor who would teach and train me one on one in his spare time. I learned more about life in our talks after class than how to defend myself. To my pastor, Dave Jamerson who has selflessly encouraged me, believed in me, giving me opportunities to grow as a communicator and leader, prayed for me, and pushed me into all God has for me.

I would also like to say thank you to my editor, Thelma Nienhuis who has helped turn this dream into a reality. Your feedback, guidance and coaching has helped me to do the impossible. To Taryn Nergaard and the team at Typewriter Creative. There is no way I could complete this project without you and your team bringing it to life.

Most importantly I want to say thank you to my family. To my amazing, beautiful, encouraging, sacrificial, and supportive wife Karen. You have put up with all my crazy dreams and believed in me when I didn't believe in myself. Your words of wisdom and insight are all throughout the pages of this book. To my four beautiful, talented, courageous daughters: Isabel, Anna, Evelyn, and Olivia. The love you have given me and the lessons you have taught me from the moment I laid eyes on you have been the difference maker in my life. You guys are my "why"! Thank you for being so patient, gracious and forgiving to a hard headed and stubborn dad that still needs to be told when to get a haircut. I couldn't have prayed for or been more proud of the young women you are growing up to be. You guys are true leaders! I know you will go further and higher in life than I could ever dreamed of.

DONNIE MAIB

Director of Olympic Sports Athletic Performance

—

UNIVERSITY OF TEXAS

Coach Donnie Maib is in his 29th year as a Strength and Conditioning Coach. He began his coaching career at the University of Colorado in 1994 where he worked with E. J. "Doc" Kreis until 1997. Coach Maib trained all varsity teams while at Colorado, where he helped many athletes obtain All-Conference as well as All-American accolades. From 1998 until the present, Coach Maib has been at the University of Texas, where he is currently the Head Coach for Athletic Performance

(Olympic Sports). As a director at Texas, Coach Maib oversees and manages 8 other performance staff and oversees 4 weight rooms. In his tenure at Texas, Coach Maib has worked with a variety of sports including Football, Women's Track, Men's and Women's Golf, Women's Soccer, Men's Tennis, and Women's Volleyball.

Most recently, Volleyball won the 2022 National Championship and Men's Tennis won the 2019 National Championship.
Volleyball has been Big XII conference championships in 2007, 2008, 2009, 2013, 2014, 2015, 2017, 2018, 2019, 2020, 2021, and 2022. In 2006, 2008, 2010, 2014, 2018, 2019, 2021, 2022 and 2023 the Men's Tennis team won the Big XII conference championship. In 2005, with Coach Maib's assistance, the University of Texas football team won the National Championship in the Rose Bowl. Additionally, under his direct supervision, Women's Track won National Championships in both their indoor and outdoor seasons in 1999. Coach Maib has had the privilege of coaching numerous Olympians, All-Conference, as well as All-American athletes, at the University of Texas. In football alone, while working alongside Coach Madden and Coach Mack Brown, there have been over 30 players drafted into the NFL in the past during his coaching era.

Coach Maib holds a 1st degree black belt in Kenpo Karate and has published a book and video entitled *Speed-Strength Training for Martial Artists.* In addition to his coaching responsibilities, Donnie started the 1st Athletic Performance Coaches Clinic for the University of Texas Athletics that brings in some of the most elite Coaches in the country to present on current topics and trends in the strength and conditioning industry. In 2020, Coach Maib launched The Team Behind the Team podcast. It is a unique and first of its kind collegiate athletics show that focuses on bringing world class experts and education on the topics of athletic performance, sports medicine, performance nutrition, sports science and mental health and wellness.

Coach Maib played football at Gallatin Senior High School where he earned All-State, All-Decade, and All-American Honors. He went on to earn a full scholarship at the University of Georgia where he lettered and started for 3 years at defensive tackle.

Donnie has been married 27 years to his wonderful wife Karen and they have four beautiful girls: Isabel, Anna, Evelyn, and Olivia.